ON JAMES BALDWIN

On
James
Baldwin
Colm
Tóibín

Brandeis University Press
Waltham, Massachusetts

Brandeis University Press

© 2024 by Colm Tóibín. All rights reserved.

The James Baldwin material is reprinted with the permission

of The James Baldwin Estate. All rights reserved.

Manufactured in the United States of America

Designed and composed in New Baskerville ITC Pro

by Mindy Basinger Hill

For permission to reproduce any of the material in this book,

contact Brandeis University Press, 415 South Street,

Waltham MA 02453, or visit brandeisuniversitypress.com

Library of Congress Cataloging-in-Publication Data

available at https://catalog.loc.gov/

cloth ISBN 978-1-68458-247-1

e-book ISBN 978-1-68458-248-8

5   4   3   2

FOR LYNNE TILLMAN

Contents

ON JAMES BALDWIN

The Pitch of Passion

———

I read James Baldwin's *Go Tell It on the Mountain* just after my eighteenth birthday, at a time when I presumed that my Catholic upbringing would soon mean little to me. During my first year at university, which I had just completed, I had told no one that I had come close to joining a seminary. Some of my memories of almost having a vocation for the priesthood were embarrassing. I wished they belonged to someone else. But now my religious feelings had not merely ended; I hoped they had been effectively erased. Such feelings, I noticed, were mostly absent from the books I was reading, the films I was watching, the plays I was going to see, the conversations I was having.

Even the religion in James Joyce's *A Portrait of the Artist as a Young Man* seemed remote. Joyce himself—and Stephen Dedalus in the novel—had attended the same university where I was now studying, but the campus had moved to the Dublin suburbs; the new buildings were glass and steel, worlds away from the intimacy of Newman House in the center of Dublin where Joyce (and Stephen) had studied. And while I had attended school retreats as Stephen did, with long sermons, we did not hear about hell as much as he did. Hell, it appeared, had died out somewhat.

I did not know much about James Baldwin. I could not have named any of his other books. I was interested in the civil rights movement in America; that might have been one reason why I had bought a copy of *Go Tell It on the Mountain*. And since the university term was over, I would have all summer to read books that were not on the curriculum.

I have no memory of being impressed or even detained much by the opening paragraph of *Go Tell It on the Mountain*. I just read it. I wonder if it was designed for that purpose: to be read without noticing the style. The sixty-two words in this opening paragraph have forty-three words with only one syllable. "Everyone had always said that John would be a preacher when he grew up, just like his father. It had been said so often that John, without ever thinking about it, had come to believe it himself. Not until the morning of his fourteenth birthday did he really begin to think about it, and by then it was already too late."

So, too, in Baldwin's short stories, as I would later discover, there is this plain, placid style. "The Rockpile" opens: "Across the street from their house, in an empty lot between two houses, stood the rockpile." "The Outing" opens: "Each summer the church gave an outing." "Sonny's Blues" opens: "I read about it in the paper, in the subway, on my way to work."

In many passages of *Go Tell It on the Mountain*, I saw when I began to study it, words are repeated. In the first page, for example, there is a deliberate repetition of words, simple words like "said," "memories," "day," "hospital," "stranger."

Most novels avoid the repetition of single words in a paragraph or a page. If a story is to be told in linear time—as though what comes next is not known and is now being revealed—then each sentence has to seem to follow from the one before. One sentence does not openly repeat the rhythm of the previous sentence or reflect it; it survives as though moving inexorably towards the future.

In *Go Tell It on the Mountain*, however, Baldwin writes as if the story is already known—"Everyone had always said," the book begins—and it's now being told again, as a folk tale might be recounted.

Words are repeated as a way of making a statement appear natural, almost casual, but also, in other passages, as they might appear in a psalm or a prayer.

Baldwin writes, for example, about John, his young protagonist, in a church in Harlem: "He did not feel it himself, the joy they felt, yet he could not doubt that it was, for them, the very bread of life—could not doubt it, that is, until it was too late to doubt."

This moment when John is overwhelmed by joy has nothing of the untidy, spontaneous tone of ordinary, secular speech. Its source is rather in the language of religious intonation, of words circling each other with an understated formality.

In an essay published two years after *Go Tell It on the Mountain*, Baldwin wrote about the sources for his prose style: "the King James Bible, the rhetoric of the store-front church, something ironic and violent and perpetually understated in Negro speech—and something of Dickens's love for bravura."

And he brought, he wrote in "Notes of a Native Son," "a

special attitude" to lofty company, to "Shakespeare, Bach, Rembrandt, to the stones of Paris, to the cathedral of Chartres, and to the Empire State Building . . . These were not really my creations; they did not contain my history . . . this was not my heritage. At the same time I had no other heritage which I could possibly hope to use—I had certainly been unfitted for the jungle and the tribe. I would have to appropriate those white centuries, I would have to make them mine."

By also appropriating the heritage of English prose, Baldwin was adapting and using not only a style but also system of thinking that used qualification, the aside, and subsequent subordinate clauses to suggest that the way towards truth was slippery, ambiguous, and easily undermined. In order to state something that was true, you had to approach it from an angle. In order to explore the weight of a word, you had to repeat the word in a different sentence. Baldwin's style could be high and grave and reflect the glittering mind; his thought was embodied in his style. His thought was subtle, ironic, but also engaged and passionate. When he needed to, he could write a plain, sharp sentence, or he could produce a high-toned effect, or he could end a long sentence with a ringing sound.

In 1962, Baldwin wrote about his adaptation of a bravura style. "I don't mean to compare myself to a couple of artists I unreservedly admire," he wrote in the *New York Times*, "Miles Davis and Ray Charles—but I would like to think that some of the people who liked my book responded to it in a way similar to the way they respond when Miles and Ray are blowing. These artists, in their very different ways, sing a kind of universal blues . . . they are telling us something of what it is like to be alive. I think I really helplessly model myself on jazz musicians and try to write the way they sound . . . I am aiming at what Henry James called 'perception at the pitch of passion.'"

Baldwin was claiming for his prose style and the structure of his novels something of the soaring, melancholy beauty of Davis and Charles; he was suggesting that the rhythms of his own diction took their bearings from the solitary pain, the uncompromising glamour which these two musicians offered the world. But just in case anyone reading him wanted thus to place him as a writer not also steeped in a literary tradition, Baldwin needed to invoke as well Henry James, the high priest of American refinement, an author known not for his passion, however pitched, but for the rigor of his controlling imagination.

Baldwin in essays and interviews needed to unloose himself from easy categories, but it was also central to his procedures as an artist that he carried in his temperament a sense of Henry James's interest in consciousness as shifting and unconfined, hidden and secretive, and he shared James's concern with language as both pure revelation and mask.

Baldwin had a fascination with eloquence itself, the rhythm pushed hard, the sharp and glorious ring of a sentence, as much as he did with the plain, declarative sentence that he placed beside his bravura style as a separate instrument, like a piano perhaps.

There are scenes in fiction that are risky to write. For example, how do you create a scene between a widow and her daughter as the daughter, already in her twenties, decides to set out from her home in a provincial place for New York City? Most likely, the mother and daughter will never meet again. What will their last conversation be like?

In the middle section of *Go Tell It on the Mountain*, Florence, whose brother Gabriel will later become John Grimes's stepfather, decides to leave her home in the South for New York. Baldwin sets this up factually and clearly as a moment in history: "In nineteen hundred, when she was twenty-six, Florence walked out through the cabin door." Before her departure, Gabriel remonstrates with her. She cannot just leave their ailing widowed mother. She responds to her brother: "'You hush,' she said, turning to him for the first time, 'she got you, ain't she?'"

What could happen next? Gabriel could shout; the mother could rise up from her bed. Some of this will happen eventually, but first there is this sentence: "This was, indeed, she realized as he dropped his eyes, the bitter, troubling point."

The bitter troubling point is that Gabriel is a drunk and a layabout. He will, in Florence's absence, be no use. But the sentence has a higher purpose than imparting that information. Its purpose is built into its tone, and its tone is in dramatic conflict with the tone Florence has been using in her speech: "You hush" and "she got you, ain't she?"

The sentence—"This was, indeed, she realized as he dropped his eyes, the bitter, troubling point"—is not Florence speaking; rather, she is responding in her mind, she is regarding the moment with poise and a sort of wisdom.

It is not as though anyone else in the novel has this kind of mind. Certainly Florence's mother doesn't, and Gabriel doesn't. Since Florence is the one about to leave, she will be in need of many ways of seeing the world, including an ability to see "the bitter, troubling point." Baldwin has handed Florence speech patterns that belong to her family and thought patterns that she has created for her own protection.

When Florence, determined to depart, tries to console her mother, Baldwin is not as interested in the words she uses as much as he is in the aura around them, the undercurrent, what is happening between Florence and her mother that is not being said. When Florence speaks, her mother does not listen: "She had granted Florence the victory—with a promptness that had the effect of making Florence, however dimly and unwillingly, wonder if her victory was real."

As Florence's circumstances change, so does the language used to reflect her new circumstances. The battle between Florence and her husband, later in the book, is rendered in ways that move beyond the ordinary and the domestic. When Baldwin writes: "She burned with longing and froze with rage," we hear his own tonal command: two words, "burned" and "longing," suggesting slow pain over a period of time. And then "froze with rage" to suggest a sharp, piercing emotion.

In *Go Tell It on the Mountain*, Baldwin is weighing words as much as emotions or moral consequences. He will not settle for a single style. There are moments where he uses his early knowledge of the Old Testament and the language of hymn and prayer and sermons. As Florence, in church, contemplates her life, with an old woman nearby calling out to her, her hands on Florence's shoulders, Baldwin writes: "And it was as though she had been hurled outward into time, where no boundaries were, for the voice was the voice of her mother, but the hands were the hands of death."

In her book *Who Set You Flowin': The African-American Migration Novel*, Farah Jasmine Griffin writes about the shifts of style in the novel, as John Grimes struggles to make a new life for himself: "Just as John vacillates between the larger white world of the stranger and the insular black world of Temple of the Fire Baptized, so too does the very language in which his story is told vacillate between that of the Western literary tradition and that of the black church."

In 1953, just before *Go Tell It on the Mountain* was published, Ralph Ellison, who had received bound galleys from the publisher, wrote to Richard Wright that Baldwin's book was "the best work on Negro religious conversion that I have seen thus far." He had a problem, however, with the style; he saw the influence of Henry James, whom Baldwin admired. "I do think," Ellison wrote, "that Baldwin could have gotten a bit closer to the material if he could have gotten rid of whatever it is that makes him feel the necessity of projecting such powerful material armored in Jamesian prose."

In a letter three months later to his friend Albert Murray, Ellison found another way of describing his disapproval of the book, wondering if all the flamboyance had a deeper source: "As for Baldwin, he doesn't know the difference between getting religion and going homo."

In *Go Tell It on the Mountain*, while Baldwin was indeed concerned with both "getting religion and going homo," he was also concerned in a larger way with conscience, with the life of the spirit rather than the material life. He did not seek to write a novel in which love might lead to marriage or in which choice and chance would do battle to dictate destiny. Nor did he seek to dramatize the tragic downfall at the hands of prejudice or the police or fate itself of a brilliant young man from Harlem. His novel is a portrait of the sinner as a young man; it dramatizes the inner life of John Grimes. John's struggle with his father is a kind of metaphor for other, more unearthly, more essential struggles, including the struggle to save his own soul.

Baldwin's novel allowed these concepts—"the inner life" and "the soul"—to appear as natural in a style that played a light, ironic tone against a fierce sympathy and seriousness.

———

What fascinated me when I read the book first was how John Grimes is allowed live in the novel at one remove from what happens to him. In a style we might call third-person intimate, Baldwin describes and invokes but does not often analyze motives or desires.

The early pages of the novel, so soaked in church ritual as spectacle, had elements that were familiar to me, as well as elements that were strange. Nothing else I had read, however, had taken experiences and emotions that I recognized and then utterly transformed them. It may have been that very mixture of styles that Farah Griffin identified, or the way in which the heightened emotion around ritual and religious belief strayed into same-sex desire, rendering the latter as unfathomable and as beguiling as the former, but more dangerous.

I came to Baldwin's novel with experiences and desires of my own that I did not understand. I did not know that all the time I spent in the local Catholic cathedral in Enniscorthy in Ireland might lodge so tenaciously in my own memory and my imagination. I did not connect my interest in religious ritual with my own pale, hidden homosexuality.

Enniscorthy cathedral, designed in the 1840s in the neo-Gothic style by the great church architect Augustus Pugin, was created to make the congregation feel wonder. On Sundays in the 1960s there were six masses, the first at seven in the morning. Often, as an altar boy, my job was to climb the winding stone stairs to the base of the spire of the cathedral and ring the bell at twenty minutes before the hour. This was to alert the town that the mass would soon be starting.

After the consecration, I would follow the priest with a paten—a round, flat, gold-colored piece of metal—placing it under the chin of those waiting to receive communion so that no tiny sliver of the sacred host would fall to the ground. I would watch as each communicant stuck out a tongue. Some stuck it out with great force; others were timid about sticking it out as if it were an intimate part of their body which they generally preferred to keep out of view.

On Thursdays at seven in the evening there was also the Boys' Confraternity in the cathedral when the host was removed from the tabernacle and displayed before us in a silver monstrance, with much burning of incense and ringing of bells to warn us to bow our heads and thump our chests lightly with our right hand as the monstrance was lifted high in the air by the priest.

And then the priest intoned these words, words that, since I can remember them sixty years later, will most likely stay with me until the end: "Death comes soon and judgment will follow. So now dear boys, examine your conscience and find out your sins."

And then the priest would become silent. The silence would echo in the vast high spaces of the cathedral.

What Baldwin managed to do with ritual like this was to surprise John Grimes with its power. This ability to be moved or even startled sets John apart from his younger brother Roy. John is the religious one, whose destiny will be played out in churches and in prayer. Or so it might seem. But, almost gently, Baldwin infuses John's faith with a current of feeling that is both distant and alarmingly close.

On the second page of the novel, John and his brother Roy recall watching a couple having sex, but even though Roy has observed them many times and "told John he had done it with some girls down the block," John "had never watched again; he had been afraid." On the next page, Elisha, who is seventeen, three years older than John, "had but lately arrived from Georgia" to the church that John and his family attend.

John "stared at Elisha all during the lesson, admiring the timbre of Elisha's voice, much deeper and manlier than his own, admiring the leanness, and grace, and strength, and darkness of Elisha in his Sunday suit, wondering if he would ever be as holy as Elisha was holy."

This is careful writing. The gaze is direct and sexual until the phrase "in his Sunday suit" which reduces the intensity and makes it seem more ordinary. The "wondering if he would ever be as holy as Elisha was holy" can be taken at face value, but it can also be read as a way of avoiding what John is really wondering. And just as John's stare is not conscious, just as John is not self-aware, a reader in 1973 in Ireland could read this as a plain, straightforward account of how John was. He is different. He looks up to Elisha because Elisha is older, because he is holy, but also because of some other appeal Elisha has, a masculine appeal, with the words there to prove it—"deeper and manlier," "leanness, and grace, and strength."

John's desires, in another scene, are almost spelled out. Clearly, he masturbates, but the word is too clinical. Instead, "he had sinned with his hands a sin that was hard to forgive." It happens when he is "in the school lavatory, alone, thinking of the boys, older, bigger, braver . . ."

The scene when Elisha dances is filled with imagery that is almost garishly sexual; it describes a body on display using terms that move far beyond the religious even while invoking the name of Jesus. "And then, like a great, black cat in trouble in the jungle, he stiffened and trembled and cried out. *Jesus, Jesus, oh Lord Jesus*."

There is no single word to describe how John feels, or who John is. He is religious, that much is certain. But what else is he?

The novel says that he was a "funny" child, not because of a hinted-at sexuality, but for ways in which he keeps his distance and, at the same times, remains alert. Early in the book, in an unsettling moment, John becomes aware "that his mother was not saying everything she meant." At another point, he sees her face changing to the face "he gave her in dreams." But no image is simple. "Between the two faces there stretched a darkness and a mystery that John feared, and that sometimes caused him to hate her."

This is a fleeting thought; it does not define John. It merely shows his mind darting and shifting. He is becoming an interpreter of silence as much as speech. John is most alive when he is most alone. His stray or deliberately unspoken thoughts create an energy at the very center of the novel.

John is thoughtful, watchful, haunted by some things, afraid of others. He is proud, but maybe that is an aspect of his fear. Sometimes his response is simple yet he is too interesting to be simple-minded. Even when he decides early in the book that he would have a life different from that of his father "or his father's fathers," it is not clear if this is fantasy or youthful ambition or a passing thought or a mixture of all these things.

While the power of prayer is apparent in Baldwin's language, it does not save his characters from having to live in history and inhabit a world that undergoes change rather than redemption. John carries the weight of being a born noticer and the weight of having been a fourteen-year-old who can undergo a religious conversion. But he also carries another weight which gives the book its structure. He carries the weight of what his parents went through.

In his book about Catholic novelists, *Maria Cross*, published in 1952, the Irish critic Conor Cruise O'Brien wrote about how those of us who come from "small and vocal communities" deal with a time and a generation that have passed: "There is for all of us a twilight zone of time, stretching back for a generation or two before we were born, which never quite belongs to the rest of history. Our elders have talked their memories into our memories until we come to possess some sense of a continuity exceeding and traversing our own individual being . . . Children of small and vocal communities are likely to possess it to a high degree and, if they are imaginative, have the power of incorporating into their own lives a significant span of time before their individual births."

In *Go Tell It on the Mountain*, it is as if John contains all that has been experienced by the previous generation. He has thus been singled out in his own world not merely because of his intelligence, or because of his sexuality, or because of his eloquence or his susceptibility to religious feeling, but also because he comes haunted by what happened before he was born. His brother Roy is not haunted in this way.

The middle sections of the novel narrate the stories of the lives of the generation before John—the children born out of wedlock, the bad marriages, the religious fervor matched by hypocrisy. Baldwin's use of shifting point of view gives us an intimate sense of John's mother Elizabeth, father Richard, stepfather Gabriel, and aunt Florence. In Baldwin, what happened a generation earlier doesn't merely foreshadow events in time present, but it infuses and animates them.

In *Go Tell It on the Mountain*, Baldwin is careful not to make the drama a simple conflict between Harlem and its hinterland, or not to allow his characters' fates to be dictated by the color of their skin. The drama comes from within. The characters have enough freedom to make decisions.

Or so it seems. In this novel, Baldwin allows one minor character to be destroyed by the police, who arrest him on false charges and beat him badly. But this character only seems minor; he is John Grimes's actual father, Richard. So, too, Gabriel's first wife Deborah is raped by a gang of White men. In another novel, she might be a minor character, but here her inner life is rendered with such care that the word "minor" ceases to mean anything. And when John himself takes a walk in Central Park and streets farther south, you realize that he is straying into perilous territory. It is an aspect of Baldwin's tact as a novelist that he allows John to come home safely. But the point has been made. All around there is danger.

Baldwin wishes to make this danger present so that the reader never underestimates how threatened his characters are and how precarious their lives. But this danger will not provide the novel with an easy plot. And even though moving the plot to the inner life of John may appear as though it is narrowing the novel's scope, it is instead fulfilling a set of principles that mattered enormously to Baldwin as an artist.

———

In 1946, the novelist Richard Wright moved to Paris. A few years earlier, in New York, Baldwin had shown him an early draft of *Go Tell It on the Mountain*. In 1948, Baldwin also moved to Paris. Even before he checked into his hotel, Baldwin was taken to the Deux Magots, a bar, where he found Wright sitting with the editors of a magazine called *Zero*. "I took this meeting as a good omen," Baldwin wrote in his essay "Alas Poor Richard," "and I could not possibly have been more wrong."

The following year Baldwin published an essay in *Zero* called "Everybody's Protest Novel." On the day the essay appeared, Baldwin walked into the Brasserie Lipp in Paris to find that Richard Wright was there. Wright called him over. He "accused me," Baldwin wrote, "of having betrayed him."

"Everybody's Protest Novel" begins with a sharp and serious attack on *Uncle Tom's Cabin* and the "protest" novel which, "so far from being disturbing," Baldwin writes, "is an accepted and comforting aspect of the American scene . . . finally we receive a very definite thrill of virtue" from reading such a book. Its "report from the pit reassures us of its reality and its darkness and our own salvation."

On the last page of the essay, Baldwin focuses his attention on Richard Wright's novel *Native Son* and the protagonist Bigger Thomas. "All of Bigger's life," Baldwin writes, "is controlled, defined by his hatred and his fear." Bigger's tragedy, he adds, is "that he admits the possibility of his being sub-human and feels constrained, therefore, to battle for his humanity according to those brutal criteria bequeathed him at his birth."

Baldwin, then, wants a character not "controlled, defined by his hatred and his fear." He seeks a novel that is not a protest against conditions already known or in which a character is locked into a battle whose terms are familiar to the reader and whose outcome can be easily imagined. Baldwin's struggle as a novelist has some of the same lofty qualities that Stephen Dedalus outlines at the end of *A Portrait of the Artist as a Young Man.*

In his biography of Baldwin, David Leeming notes that Baldwin read James Joyce in Paris in 1950 while he was working on *Go Tell It on the Mountain.* "The connections between Joyce's flight from Ireland and his own from Harlem were certainly not lost on him," Leeming writes, pointing out also that both Baldwin and Dedalus were young artists troubled by their religious backgrounds. Both Baldwin and Joyce, despite their exile and also because of it, wrote intense first novels about the places they came from, with versions of themselves as sensitive young men dealing with family and religion, attempting to outsoar their circumstances.

Thus, Joyce's *A Portrait of the Artist as a Young Man* was not lost on Baldwin. The need to do battle with religion and his own oppressed nation; the need to go into exile; the need to create a personal voice and personal mode of perception; these became Baldwin's needs as much as they'd been Joyce's. "What I mainly learned [in France]," Baldwin later said, in an interview with the *Transatlantic Review,* "was about my own country, my own past, and about my own language. Joyce accepted silence, exile and cunning as a system which would sustain his life, and I've had to accept it too—incidentally, silence is the hardest part to understand."

Go Tell It on the Mountain is as much a landmark in American writing as Joyce's collection of stories *Dubliners* was in Ireland. *Dubliners* refused to allow its characters to have their destiny shaped directly by Irish history or the struggle for land or ghosts of the Famine dead or the British presence in Ireland. Both Joyce's characters and Baldwin's characters suffer because of what is within them.

In placing the very nature of his characters, their inner demons, at the center, Baldwin refused to write a parable of race relations. But there is one other aspect of Joyce that may have interested Baldwin. Joyce's novel *Ulysses* is set in 1904 but written in the period between 1914 and 1921. Since that latter period was a time of ferment and destruction in Ireland—the 1916 Rebellion, for example, followed by the Irish War of Independence—Joyce could have made his novel a drama in which Irish characters were controlled by hatred and fear and sought to battle for their humanity against English domination.

Instead, Joyce wrote his novel in competing styles, relishing the freedom offered by city life on a day in midsummer. If his characters are oppressed, then their oppression emerges as linguistic performance and comic interludes. History is the comedy from which his characters are trying to awake. In the meantime, there is a joke to make, a drink to have, and an exuberant parody of the systems of prose-making most in vogue in Ireland and in England, not to speak of the Odyssey.

Episode 10 of *Ulysses* is called "Wandering Rocks"; its action takes place in the center of Dublin using nineteen different scenes to show what various characters are doing at three o'clock in the afternoon. It uses a system of spliced narrative, with some characters appearing a number of times, others only once. What is notable about the episode is its ordinariness. Nobody says anything especially interesting. Nothing dramatic occurs. The drama arises from the way that time and city space are handled, how experience is edited, chopped up, and put back together again.

This is interrupted by a single sentence about a third of the way into the episode: "The gates of the drive opened wide to give egress to the viceregal cavalcade." The lord-lieutenant, who travels with an entourage in this cavalcade, is the King's representative in Ireland. He is, in theory at least, the most powerful person in the country. Soon, when "Clatter of horse-hoofs sounded from the air," a number of Dubliners hear it, but when one asks what the sound was: "The lord lieutenant-general and general governor of Ireland, John Wyse Nolan answered from the stairfoot." Immediately, the narrative cuts away from this scene.

What is significant here is that, in a novel filled with quips and sour remarks, John Wyse Nolan, a minor character in the book, has nothing smart or funny or disrespectful to say about the cavalcade. And, unlike other events in *Ulysses* such as the Ascot Gold Cup or the explosion on the *General Slocum* in New York harbor, this cavalcade did not, in fact, take place on or near June 16, 1904, the date on which the novel, famous for its verisimilitude, takes place.

Joyce chose to invent it not because he needed a dramatization of a display of power and pomp but as the dramatization of a display of weakness, indifference. No one in the novel feels anything much at the sight of the King's representatives in Ireland. It is as though the King's day has already passed.

While the humblest citizen is allowed to speak in this episode, the novel does not enter the carriage itself. The English people being transported across the city are silent. They are not described. A ghost has wandered by carriage through a busy city on an ordinary afternoon.

It might have been tempting to make this scene into one of high drama, in which Irish nationalist tempers flared at the sight of the cavalcade. But the lack of patriotic response to the cavalcade in the novel is not sociological; it is not a way of telling the reader how passive Dubliners were in 1904. Rather, it is a way of freeing the novel and its characters from the constraints of fixed response. They are not "controlled or defined by their hatred or their fear."

If a novel set in Dublin in 1904 or in Harlem in the late 1940s does not openly dramatize the conflict between power and powerlessness, if it does not have epic scenes and a sense of panorama, what does it do?

It might be easy to misread *Go Tell It on the Mountain* as a set of brilliant vignettes and flashbacks. It focuses intensely on the private lives of a few characters. It takes the world of John Grimes as intrinsically interesting and dramatic, making clear that he and his family do not need the intrusion of White America into their story to make it worth telling.

In Derek Walcott's poem "The Schooner Flight," his protagonist is "either nobody, or I'm a nation." John Grimes is a nation.

When Leopold Bloom in James Joyce's *Ulysses* is asked what a nation is, he replies "the same people in the same place," and then adds "or the same people in different places." In *Go Tell It on the Mountain*, Harlem is both the same place where the characters live now and a place many of them have come to, having lived in a different place. Some of the older characters—John's mother and his stepfather Gabriel and his aunt Florence—came from the South to New York. Much of the action in the book occurs in the South before John's birth. Gradually, the novel emerges as a book that is, in one of its manifestations, about the Great Migration.

I did not notice this when I first read the book.

———

In Ireland, emigration was part of life enough to be surrounded by silence. Half a million people left the country between 1945 and 1960, when the population of the country was only three million. Those who had gone to England sometimes visited in the summer; those who had gone to America or Australia did not often come back. And if they did return, the people who had stayed behind were unsure how to speak to them or treat them. There was a sense that once you left, you belonged neither in the place you had gone to or the place you might have once called home.

It is hard to describe the unruffled atmosphere in our town in the years when I was growing up. No one much came from outside, not even ideas. Voting patterns were stable. In the Catholic graveyard just outside the town my four grandparents were buried, as my parents would be, and my aunts and uncles and cousins. All of them lived their lives in the town. The town may have been haunted by history and unsettled by emigration, but it felt a most solid, rooted place. And we had controlled the country since independence in 1922. We would not need to wait for change or hope for deliverance.

There was a quiet background noise that might have been mistaken for disruption, but the disruption had all happened in the past—in the 1916 Rebellion, in the Great Famine, and in the doomed Rebellion of 1798 that left the town burning.

At home, we had an old copy of John and Michael Banim's novel *The Croppy*, first published in 1828, in which there was an extraordinary account of Enniscorthy on fire in the summer of 1798: "the majority of the shrieking inhabitants—the young, the old—the wealthy, the needy—beauty and deformity, flew pell-mell with the retreating garrison, through scorching flames . . . Hundreds of burning dwellings sent masses of fire to surcharge the already sultry atmosphere. Until in the lower streets of Enniscorthy, overhung by clouds of smoke, and strewed with hot ashes, respiration became painful, and exertion difficult . . . All was shout, shriek, and clamor, while overhead roared the ravenous flames."

This happened one hundred and fifty-seven years before I was born. The rebellion became the subject of popular ballads as well as scenes in novels. From our house, we could see Vinegar Hill, where the last battle of the 1798 Rebellion took place. Around us were the villages named in the ballads. Sometimes, it meant nothing; at other times it seemed as though it had never been fully consigned to the past. When my parents went to a play about the Rebellion, the actors sat among the audience and often let out big rebel shouts or warnings. This was perhaps a fitting way to dramatize the Rebellion.

In the background of the town's life was a notion that some great catastrophe had once occurred. We were alert to its powerful and glowing aftermath, but not all the time. Mostly, things were ordinary.

———

It might be possible to argue that this was far from the world out of which Baldwin came. But it is important to make clear that, in certain and uncertain ways, while Harlem was a powder keg, it had its own stability, its own ordinariness. According to biographer Herb Boyd, Baldwin told the anthropologist Margaret Mead: "When I grew up we lived in what was recognized as a neighborhood. Everybody vaguely knew everybody else. We knew the man who ran the drugstore, the man who ran the butcher shop." Baldwin was also alert to the class divisions within the Black community in Harlem. "You see," he told interviewer Julius Lester for the *New York Times* in 1984, "there were two Harlems. There were those who lived in Sugar Hill and there was the Hollow, where we lived. I was just a ragged, funky black shoeshine boy and was afraid of the people on the Hill, who, for their part, didn't want to have anything to do with me."

In 1930, when Baldwin was six, James Weldon Johnson published his book *Black Manhattan*. Johnson had come from Florida to New York around the turn of the century. With his brother, he wrote "Lift Every Voice and Sing," which became an anthem for Black Americans. When Teddy Roosevelt was president, in 1906 Johnson was appointed US consul to Venezuela and then in 1909 to Nicaragua. (He had written the lyrics for Roosevelt's campaign song.)

"It should be noted," Johnson wrote in *Black Manhattan*, "that Harlem was taken over without violence." As millions of Black people migrated from the South to cities in the North, the resentment, in places such as Chicago, Cleveland, and Detroit, spilled over into violence. "Not since the riot of 1900," Johnson wrote, "has New York witnessed, except for minor incidents, any interracial disturbances. Not even in the summer of 1919 . . . not even in this period of massacre did New York, with more than a hundred thousand Negroes grouped together in Harlem, lose its equanimity."

"At any rate," he continued, "there is no longer any apparent feeling against the occupancy of Harlem by Negroes. Within the past five years the colony has expanded to the south, the north, and the west." This, he added, "has taken place without any physical opposition, or even any considerable outbreak of antagonistic public sentiment . . . the Negro's situation in Harlem is without precedent in all his history in New York; never before has he been so securely anchored . . . never before has he had so well established a community life."

In 1948 when Baldwin published the essay "The Harlem Ghetto" in *Commentary*, his earliest piece for a national magazine, his view of Harlem was less sanguine: "All over Harlem now," he wrote, "there is felt the same bitter expectancy with which, in my childhood, we awaited winter: it is coming and it will be hard; there is nothing anyone can do about it."

And then, after a paragraph break, he continued: "All of Harlem is pervaded by a sense of congestion, rather like the insistent, maddening, claustrophobic pounding in the skull that comes from trying to breathe in a very small room with all the windows shut. Yet the white man walking through Harlem is not at all likely to find it sinister or more wretched than any other slum."

Twelve years later in an essay in *Esquire*, Baldwin contemplated the role of the police in Harlem: "They represent the force of the white world, and that world's real intentions are, simply, for that world's criminal profit and ease, to keep the black man corralled up here, in his place. The badge, the gun in the holster, and the swinging club make vivid what will happen should his rebellion become overt."

The businesses in Harlem were mainly owned by Whites. The historian John Henrik Clarke wrote of Harlem: "It is owned and controlled by outsiders. It is a black community with a white economic heartbeat."

When Baldwin was ten, a riot broke out in Harlem when a Puerto Rican youth was arrested, accused of shoplifting. It was, as one historian pointed out, a riot against the White shop-owning class as much as the racist police. In *Or Does It Explode?*, Cheryl Greenberg wrote: "By the end of the night 697 plate glass windows in some 300 business establishments were shattered . . . the police had detained 121 people, and 57 civilians and 7 police had been injured. And most tragically, Lloyd Hobbs, a black schoolboy on his way home from the cinema, had been shot and killed by the police."

Ten years later, another riot began in Harlem, the riot that would coincide with the funeral of James Baldwin's father, a few days after Baldwin's youngest sister was born. It was this riot that would connect the personal and the political for him as he produced one of his greatest essays, "Notes of a Native Son," published in *Harper's* in 1955.

In his essay "Tradition and the Individual Talent," T. S. Eliot wrote about "the historical sense, which we may call nearly indispensable to any one who would continue to be a poet beyond his twenty-fifth year; and the historical sense involves a perception, not only of the pastness of the past, but of its presence."

For Baldwin, the past was bound up with place, and since his sense of place was bound up with displacement, the past did not come simply. What is strange is how stories from the past represent the very center of *Go Tell It on the Mountain*, enough to make it a novel about how the displacement caused by the Great Migration entered into the spirit of these characters and their relationships.

The novel has a shadow world where the past happened, where the earlier generation came from, and where much that was unresolved had been left behind. The novel dramatizes what the Great Migration did to the souls of a number of characters living in Harlem as the novel opens.

For a writer, there is nothing more potent than a lost place, somewhere that was fully known and intensely inhabited by the previous generation, and that is spoken about enough to inhabit the imagination as though it were memory. Baldwin's handling of the lost place gives the novel much of its power.

That lost place in *Go Tell It on the Mountain* is the American South. "A black boy born in New York's Harlem in 1924," Baldwin wrote in *Esquire* in 1980, "was born of southerners who had but lately been driven from land, and therefore was born into a southern community."

———

In an interview in the *New York Post* in 1938, Richard Wright, who was born in 1908 on a Mississippi plantation, spoke about the lure of the North for those in the American South: "The compulsion of Negro life in the Deep South is to get up and travel, to get North. Other Negroes come back and tell you that a Negro in the North is treated like a human being and, if you want certain things, you get up and travel hundreds of miles."

Seven years later, Wright said in another interview: "Urbanization brings the southern Negro within the living orbit of the nation for the first time. It brings him into contact with literacy, with democratic ideas, makes him conscious of his relation to the nation. The war [the Second World War] has accelerated the northward drift, and has speeded up the progress of the Negro. But it has been an unconscious process—like an express train stirring up dry leaves."

In the same year, in the essay "Black Boy and Reading," Wright wrote about his own journey north: "Living in the South doomed me to look always through eyes which the South had given me, and bewilderment and fear made me mute and afraid. But after I left the South luck gave me other eyes, new eyes with which to look at the meaning of what I'd live through. I came North in my 19th year, filled with the hunger to know."

This passage by Wright appears in the "restored edition" of *Black Boy*:

I was leaving the South to fling myself into an unknown . . . I was taking a part of the South to transplant in alien soil, to see if it could grow differently, if it could drink of new and cool rains, bend in strange winds, respond to the warmth of other suns and, perhaps, to bloom.

One of Wright's phrases there gives Isabel Wilkerson the title of her book *The Warmth of Other Suns: The Epic Story of America's Great Migration.*

"It was during the First World War," she wrote, "that a silent pilgrimage took its first steps within the borders of this country. . . . Historians would come to call it the Great Migration. It would become perhaps the biggest underreported story of the twentieth century. . . . Over the course of six decades, some six million black southerners left the land of their forefathers."

The imprint of the Great Migration "is everywhere in urban life . . . the language and music of urban America that sprang from the blues that came with the migrants. . . . People as diverse as James Baldwin and Michelle Obama, Miles Davis and Toni Morrison, Spike Lee and Denzel Washington . . . were all products of the Great Migration. They were all children whose life chances were altered because a parent or grandparent had made the hard decision to leave."

The bare facts of what happened are set out in dry tones in

Report of the National Advisory Commission on Civil Disorders, published on March 1, 1968: "In 1910, 91 percent of the Nation's 9.8 million Negroes lived in the South. Twenty-seven percent of American Negroes lived in cities of 2,500 persons or more, as compared to 49 percent of the Nation's white population.

"By 1966, the Negro population had increased to 21.5 million, and two significant geographic shifts had taken place. The proportion of Negroes living in the South had dropped to 55 percent, and about 69 percent of all Negroes lived in metropolitan areas compared to 64 percent for whites. While the total Negro population more than doubled from 1910 to 1966, the number living in cities rose over fivefold (from 2.7 million to 14.8 million) and the number outside the South rose elevenfold (from 885,000 to 9.7 million)."

This is put more sonorously by Langston Hughes in his poem "One Way Ticket":

I pick up my life
And take it on the train
To Los Angeles, Bakersfield,
Seattle, Oakland, Salt Lake,
Any place that is
North and West—
And not South.

———

Fiction and poetry and songs may be the best ways to explore the estrangement that comes with displacement; the idea that what is missing has become almost unnamable but stays in the air—palpable, potent—is part of the lure of this subject for a writer.

It cannot be retrieved except in images, the more disparate the more powerful.

In *Ulysses*, while James Joyce, in exile from Dublin, wrote about the city he remembered, the city he had lost, he wrote most intensely about his father's city. He imagined his father's life. The jokes in the book were his father's. Most of the characters came from his father's generation. Of his father, he wrote: "The humor of *Ulysses* is his; its people are his friends. The book is his spittin' image."

Go Tell It on the Mountain explores the Great Migration as it affects the lives of two generations, the earlier one born in the South, the later one living in the North, but in the South's shadow, as if the younger characters had almost known, almost experienced, a time before they themselves came into being.

And the language of the book often feels as if it too had known an earlier time, as if it took its bearing from a rhetoric that had been heard in a more treacherous place than Harlem, a place from which people sought to escape, as though escape were a kind of deliverance. When John's aunt Florence appears in the church at the very end of section one of the novel, Baldwin writes: "John knew that it was the hand of the Lord that had led her to this place, and his heart grew cold. The Lord was riding on the wind tonight. What might that wind have spoken before the morning came?"

John's friend Elisha "had been saved at the age of eleven in the improbable fields down south." Part of his mystery, and perhaps even part of his glamour, is the fact that he comes from a place that John can only imagine.

Among the photographs in John's family's possession is one of Aunt Florence "when she had just come North" and another of his father as a young preacher who was married to a woman called Deborah who had died in the South. "If she had lived, John thought, then he would never have been born; his father would never have come North and met his mother." He doesn't yet know that Gabriel is his stepfather, not his biological father.

That first wife of Gabriel's, "this shadowy woman, dead so many years, whose name he knew had been Deborah, held in the fastness of her tomb, it seemed to John, the key to all those mysteries he so longed to unlock. It was she who had known his father in a life where John was not, in a country he had never seen."

But it is a country he knows about. "John had read about the things white people did to colored people; how in the South, where his parents came from, white people cheated them of their wages, and burned them, and shot them—and did worse things, said his father, which the tongue could not endure to utter."

Part of the reason why John is so intrigued by the South is that Gabriel's power seems to have diminished when he moved north. He "had once had a mighty reputation; but all this, it seemed, had changed since he had left the South."

Slowly, events that took place in the South come to haunt the book, as they haunt John's imagination, as they offer a more fervid tone to the narrative. When Deborah was taken into the fields and raped by many White men, Deborah's father threatened that he would kill these men, and he was left for dead by them. Then everyone, including Gabriel's mother and his sister, "had shut their doors, praying and waiting, for it was said that the white folks would come tonight and set fire to all the houses, as they had done before."

Baldwin has a special tone to describe the Southern night. A special eloquence, a way of balancing his sentences, using elaborate description and then a plain statement—moving from human feelings to ones that embrace the Almighty, creating an atmosphere that is unearthly and ominous: "In the night that pressed outside they heard only the horse's hoofs, which did not stop; there was not the laughter they would have heard had there been many coming on this road, and no calling out of curses, and no one crying for mercy to white men, or to God."

"Which did not stop" makes clear that this is happening in real time, that "the night that pressed outside" is not a metaphor. "And no calling out of curses" has echoes of lines in the King James Bible.

The South is not merely a place of fear, but a place where slavery exists in living memory. John's father's mother had grown up as a slave, as "a field worker, for she was very tall and strong; and by and by she had married and raised children, all of whom had been taken from her, one by sickness and two by auction; and one, whom she had not been allowed to call her own, had been raised in the master's house."

From this place, people would disappear, would be gone by morning on their journey North. Florence's father, whom she scarcely remembered, had departed that way one morning not many months after the birth of her brother Gabriel. "And not only her father; every day she heard that another man or woman had said farewell to this iron earth and sky and started on the journey North."

For some, the North meant freedom, but not for John's grandmother, who "had no wish to go North where, she said, wickedness dwelt and death rode mighty through the streets."

For Elizabeth, John's mother, who would become Gabriel's second wife, "there was not, after all, a great difference between the world of the North and that of the South which she had fled; there was only this difference: the North promised more. And this similarity: what it promised it did not give, and what it gave, at length and grudgingly with one hand, it took back with the other."

In his second autobiography *American Hunger*, Richard Wright wrote even more forcefully about the disillusion and indeed the shock that came with migration: "My first glimpse of the flat black stretches of Chicago depressed and dismayed me, mocked all my fantasies. Chicago seemed an unreal city whose mythical houses were built on slabs of black coal wreathed in palls of grey smoke. . . . The din of the city entered my consciousness, entered to remain for years to come."

———

Two years after *Go Tell It on the Mountain* appeared, Baldwin published an account of how his father, who died on July 29, 1943, came to resemble the figure of Gabriel in the novel. "No one, including my father, seems to have known exactly how old he was . . . He was of the first generation of free men. He, along with thousands of other Negroes, came North after 1919 and I was part of that generation which had never seen the landscape of what Negroes sometimes call the Old Country."

David Leeming, in his biography of Baldwin, writes: "During the summer of 1957 Baldwin talked incessantly about the South, his fear of it and his sense of his own vulnerability in relation to it." He was about to make his first visit there.

In the essay "Nobody Knows My Name: A Letter from the South," Baldwin notes that, as he was preparing to set out, he was cautioned by a friend to "remember that Southern Negroes had endured things I could not imagine" and was warned of "the tension that might exist between blacks of the South and the black reporter from the North." He is told "that it might be a good idea to arrive in Charlotte, North Carolina, the first stop on the itinerary, during the day rather than at night."

Before he ever travelled south, Baldwin has experienced its atmosphere by listening to the stories told with a particular intensity and curiosity, and before experiencing the dangers, he has imagined them in one of the most chillingly powerful episodes in *Go Tell It on the Mountain*.

This is a scene when Gabriel unexpectedly meets Royal, his son by a woman other than his wife, on a night when there has been a lynching. At first, as Gabriel walks alone, "white men stood in groups of half a dozen. As he passed each group, silence fell, and they watched him insolently, itching to kill; but he said nothing, bowing his head, and they knew, anyway, that he was a preacher. There were no black men on the streets at all, save him."

When he meets Royal, the tone becomes more ominous: "Then the corner on which they stood seemed suddenly to rock with the weight of mortal danger. It seemed for a moment, as they stood there, that death and destruction rushed towards them: two black men alone in the dark and silent town where white men prowled like lions—what mercy could they hope for, should they be found here, talking together?"

In "Nobody Knows My Name," Baldwin came, then, to the place that he had imagined: "In the fall of last year, my plane hovered over the rust-red earth of Georgia. I was past thirty, and I had never seen this land before."

For Baldwin, as he contemplated the gap between the North and the South, paradox and irony were often wrapped around bald binaries. The Northern White person, Baldwin wrote in 1960, "never sees Negroes. Southerners see them all the time. Northerners never think about them whereas Southerners are never really thinking of anything else. Negroes are, therefore, ignored in the North and are under surveillance in the South, and suffer hideously in both places. Neither the Southerner nor the Northerner is able to look on the Negro simply as a man."

The idea of what it would mean to be a man, or what it would take, under these pressures, would become one of Baldwin's great subjects.

Crying Holy

In an essay published after Richard Wright's death, James Baldwin praised a story by Wright, originally a radio play, called "Man of All Work." It was written, Baldwin notes, "with beautiful spite and accuracy [about] the private lives of the master race." It begins with a poor Black couple, Carl and Lucy. Lucy has just had her second child and Carl can't get work. The rent is overdue. And when they see an ad for a cook and housekeeper, Carl, who is "a trained army cook," decides to dress in his wife's clothes and apply for the job.

"I can pass," he says. When Lucy remonstrates with him, he replies: "Who looks at us colored people anyhow? We all look alike to white people." And later he adds: "I can act good enough to fool white folks." Carl gets the job, and only the little girl in the White household notices anything strange. The woman of the house asks her husband: "How does she look? How old is she?" The husband replies: "Didn't ask her. Didn't notice her."

Soon, the mistress, in a creepy scene in the bathroom, hits on her new housekeeper, much to her/his consternation. And then the husband, who has harassed and sexually abused the previous housekeeper, begins to harass the new one. Neither husband nor wife has any inkling that their new housekeeper is a man. (Even when the husband says "you're as strong as a man," he doesn't understand what he is saying.) They know he is Black, however and, in the story, this knowledge means they don't have to pay any close attention to him, even as they set out to seduce him.

Baldwin called the story "a tight, raging, diamond-hard exercise in irony." The irony arises from the idea that this most straight White couple is only passing for straight. The wife obviously likes having her back scrubbed and her naked body checked out by another woman. This is what she did with the previous Black housekeeper and wants to do again with the new one. The husband finds himself chasing a Black man around the room with a view to having sex with him.

But there is a deeper, more unsettling irony that centers on the idea of who poses and who passes, whose voice is hidden and who gets to identify themselves.

In 1961 a book appeared that intensified these questions. It was called *Black Like Me*, written by a progressive journalist, John Howard Griffin. Commissioned and first serialized in *Sepia*, a magazine with a mainly Black readership, it was an account by a White man of what it was like to be Black in the South. It was written firsthand, as it were, since Griffin darkened the color of his skin and posed as Black and usually passed as Black.

The book was published in hardcover and paperback at the same time, unusual then as now; it sold millions of copies and made Griffin a celebrity for a while. It was reviewed favorably in most of the mainstream press in America, although it was ignored by most papers in the South. (In 1964, it was made into a movie which was less warmly received. Brendan Gill, in the *New Yorker*, wrote that the actor playing Griffin had "very light blue eyes, the accent of a New England grocer and he wouldn't have fooled me for a moment.")

Strangely, in Ireland, the book was read in many households. It was the choice of a Catholic book club to which good Catholic families like mine had subscribed. (The only other book I can remember from the club was called *The Scarlet Pimpernel of the Vatican*, an account of an Irish priest who saved lives in the Second World War, using the Vatican as an exit route.) I read *Black Like Me*, aged fourteen or fifteen, as did some of my friends to whose houses the same book had arrived.

Recently, I went to check two moments in the book, two details. Could my memory be accurate after fifty-five years?

The first is when our narrator has befriended a Black man who shines shoes, and has admitted that he really is White. And his disguise, or his new skin tone, works well, fools everyone, until his friend, the shoeshine, points to the hair on the back of his hands and says this gives the game away. The writer goes and shaves the back of his hands.

That scene is still there. I have no idea why I remember it.

I recall being convinced by the book, not just by the facts reported and the stories recounted and the observations made, but also by the initial idea—that a White man passing for Black might be a good witness to what it was like to be Black in those places at that time. I am certain that no one around me questioned the value of Griffin's journey or the seriousness of his mission.

Griffin was idealistic and almost innocent. He told an editor that "the best way to find out if we had second-class citizens and what their plight was would be to become one of them."

When he first meets the man who works as a shoeshine—a time when he is walking the streets of New Orleans as a Black man, getting used to his new identity—he writes: "The shine boy was an elderly man, large, keenly intelligent and a good talker. He had lost a leg during World War I. He showed none of the obsequiousness of the Southern Negro, but was polite and easy to know. (Not that I had any illusion that I knew him, for he was too astute to allow any white man that privilege.)"

It is hard not to wonder about this: How can Griffin make such a glib assertion?

As a Black man hitchhiking, Griffin finds out why White men will give him a ride at night and not in the day. And this is the second thing from the book that I remembered after all the years: "A man will reveal himself in the dark, which gives the illusion of anonymity, more than he will in the bright light. Some were shamelessly open, some shamelessly subtle. All showed morbid curiosity about the sexual life of the Negro. . . . They carried the conversation into depths of depravity."

We are back in the world of Richard Wright's story "Man of All Work" in which a figure passing as a Black woman or a Black man becomes a catalyst, a vehicle, a way to discover that the racial prejudices of some White people are weirdly bound up with their sexual dreams.

Part of the interest of the book when I first read it was John Howard Griffin's own fascination with his new appearance, as though he were enacting a light version of *Dr. Jekyll and*

Mr. Hyde. When he looks in the mirror in the early period of his transformation, he sees that "the face and shoulder of a stranger—a fierce, bald, very dark Negro—glared at me from the glass. He in no way resembled me . . . I became two men, the observing one and the one who panicked, who felt Negroid even in the depths of his entrails . . . I had tampered with the mystery of existence and I had lost the sense of my own being. This is what devastated me."

Griffin, in his new guise, when he is not looking at himself in the mirror, writes graphically about what it is like to travel from New Orleans into the state of Mississippi, sitting at the back of the bus, with the Blacks prevented by the driver from using the bathroom when the bus stops for a break.

Griffin is alone. Like a figure in a crime thriller, he walks the mean streets with mysterious purpose. He stays in dingy places. He feels fear. He can't go into many restaurants. Some White people stare at him with hatred.

There are moments, however, when he is too involved with his own witness statement. When he goes looking for a job, he writes, "I wanted to discover what sort of work an educated Negro, nicely dressed, could find." But, surely, he would get a more accurate version of this by asking people and listening to their answers? And too early in the book he appears ready to let us know about "Negroes," as though he is one: "The Negro often dreams of things separated from him only by a door, knowing that he is forever cut off from experiencing them."

But this is to miss the point of his book and the moment in which it was written. Griffin doesn't dwell too much on his deep-rooted Catholicism or boast about his own decency, but these become essential elements in his narrative. The most powerful moment comes when he gets a ride with a White man who asks about his wife. "You got a pretty wife?" And then: "She ever had it from a white man?" And soon the man says that he has employed many Black women. "And I guarantee you, I've had it in every one of them before they ever got on the payroll . . . If they don't put out they don't get the job . . . We figure we're doing you people a favor to get some white blood in your kids."

Griffin's response is cold and eloquent and disgusted, as it is when the same man talks about what they do to Black troublemakers: "We either ship them off to the pen or kill them."

"He spoke in a tone," Griffin writes, "that sickened me, casual, merciless. I looked at him. His decent blue eyes turned yellow. I knew that nothing could touch him to have mercy once he decided a Negro should be 'taught a lesson.' The immensity of it terrified me. But it caught him up like a lust now. He entertained it, his voice unctuous with pleasure and cruelty. The highway stretched deserted through the swamp forests."

This tone of high moral seriousness mattered when *Black Like Me* was published. It meant that Griffin could appear on TV talk shows, including *The Mike Wallace Show*, with news that he felt was vitally important for his fellow Americans to hear. In the years after the book was published, he gave more than a thousand lectures to mostly White college audiences. In one that was recorded on April 22, 1964, at Ball State University in Indiana, we can note his gravity, how slowly he speaks as though every word must be taken in and weighed, how he makes clear he is talking about things that are wrong and he knows they are wrong because he went to find out himself. Nothing he says can be denied.

But there are other ways of considering this story, including one that is ironic and picaresque. *Black No More*, by the African American writer and journalist George S. Schuyler, published in 1931, is a brilliant burlesque of a novel about race. It concerns a young man in Harlem who is rebuffed by a beautiful White girl from Atlanta and determines to do what he can to win her. This includes taking advantage of a new treatment that will make Black people into Whites. "It looked as though science was to succeed where the Civil War had failed . . . Sure, it was taking a chance, but think of getting white in three days! . . . As a white man he could go anywhere . . ." The operation to make this transformation is rather more arduous than that undergone by John Howard Griffin, but the rewards are great, or so we are led to believe as our hero makes his way down Broadway with a White girl, "with a feeling of absolute freedom and sureness. No one looked at him curiously because he was with a white girl . . . Gee, it was great!"

———

At the time I read James Baldwin's *Go Tell It on the Mountain* in 1973, *Black Like Me* was the only other book I had read about race in America. In an epilogue, written later, Griffin makes clear he spent time with civil rights leaders, including Martin Luther King Jr., after his book was written. He lists a good number of activists, but the list doesn't include James Baldwin. And in Baldwin's published writings I can find no reference to John Howard Griffin and his book.

In 1959, the same year as Griffin's investigation began, Baldwin published "A Letter from the South: Nobody Knows My Name" in the *Partisan Review*. *Nobody Knows My Name* became the title of his second essay collection, published in 1961. Two years later, he published two long essays in a book with the title *The Fire Next Time*.

These essays appeared first in mainstream magazines; they were written for deadlines. But what is strange now, more than half a century later, is that they have lost nothing of their original brilliance.

The essays are personal and passionate and angry. The tone can also be wise, analytical, knowing, clued-in and ironic, relishing nuance, ambiguity, and paradox. What gives these pieces such life after all these years is the way in which Baldwin's intelligence and his prose style match each other. Some of the essays' power also arises, of course, from the urgency of their moment. They were written when there was a great deal at stake. In a period of competing voices, speaking a difficult truth became both a risk and a burning necessity.

Writing itself—well-made sentences, cadences sonorous and shaped, command of competing tones—could become, in such a time, a sort of politics. The Irish poet Seamus Heaney has spoken of what poetry, for example, can do in a time of conflict, as in Northern Ireland during the Troubles. "All of us, Protestant poets, Catholic poets," he said in an interview, "probably had some notion that a good poem was 'a paradigm of good politics,' a site of energy and tension and possibility, a truth-telling arena but not a killing field. And without being explicit about it, either to ourselves or to one another, we probably felt that if we as poets couldn't do something transformative or creative with all that we were a part of, then it was a poor lookout for everybody."

Baldwin began writing in a period when it was not considered strange that a White writer masquerading as Black could be the best witness to the lives of Black people. Who else could speak?, it might have been asked.

It was as though, in order to find out about conditions in Ireland, someone English would be best equipped, someone who could learn to speak with an Irish accent, acquire some red hair and freckles and drink a load of Guinness. Or in order to find out how gay people felt, someone straight might arrive at the party.

Such proposals would be preposterous, unthinkable, a joke. But Griffin was an honorable man who believed that he would be a good witness, better perhaps than those who lived through the injustice all their lives and did not have to impersonate anyone to experience it.

———

In 2006, I went to teach for a few months at Stanford University where my immediate boss was the Irish poet Eavan Boland, whom I had known slightly in Dublin. She had a formidable intelligence and a passionate response to poetry. She did not suffer fools gladly, and I had often wondered over the years, when I bumped into her at literary events in Dublin, if I was among the fools. She often peered at me.

It did not help that there was a poem by her that I loved and could recite. It was an early poem that she had come close to repudiating. In my first week at Stanford, there was a dinner at which she and I spoke of some Irish poems that we both admired. Then I made the mistake of mentioning that poem by her. (It is called "Song.") I may even have begun to recite it. Eavan looked at me witheringly—something she could do with great effect—and turned to one of the other guests. I wondered how my time at Stanford was going to go.

In conversation, Eavan avoided irony or easy humor or any form of banter, often displaying a tone that was unusually direct and serious. Behind the steeliness, there was kindness and humor. But it took me a while to work that out.

Soon, I noticed something about Eavan's voice and style of speaking—a mixture of formality with grace and charm. She often sounded uncannily like Mary Robinson, who had been president of Ireland from 1990 to 1997. During her campaign for the presidency, Robinson had noticeably softened her lawyerly, considered tone. She had begun to exude a careful way of listening and paying attention, a kind of warmth.

It really was remarkable how close Eavan sounded to Robinson, not just the voice, but the inflections, the diction. I knew that she and Robinson had been friends because she had dedicated a poem to Robinson. But, as the months went on, I learned that they had known one another as students and that the friendship had deepened as they both married and settled in Dublin, Mary Robinson becoming a human rights lawyer, Eavan a poet.

I learned too how much Eavan was involved as Mary Robinson sought to reimagine the role of president. Eavan had even written speeches for Mary Robinson, I learned, and parts of speeches, including the most famous ones.

In her essays and poems, Eavan wrote about Ireland, its history of loss and dispossession, its emigrants, its women erased from official history. Some of her poems were passionate interventions. She found a style filled with a sympathy that complemented her eloquence and her technical skills as a poet.

The mixture in her work—the journey with two maps, as Eavan called it, between the interior life and history—lent Eavan her fame as a poet. Mary Robinson's journey was also one with two maps—one map charted her interest in the law and social change, but the other was uncharted territory, surrounded by silence, the legacy of emigration, dispossession, and discrimination against women in Ireland.

In her official residence, once she was elected, Mary Robinson lit a lamp and placed it in a window. It was for those who had left Ireland seeking a life elsewhere, those who had been excluded from the narrative of life in Ireland.

On August 25, 2014, Eavan Boland published a poem in the *New Yorker* called "The Lost Art of Letter Writing." It was about Irish emigrants writing home, but it was not about the sadness of these letters, or a sense of homesickness in them, but rather about what their senders wished to recover and rediscover ("always asking after what they kept losing") and how, over the years, an art such as letter writing can be lost "when it no longer knows / How to teach a sorrow to speak."

This poem was tentative, exploratory, uncertain about where its own argument might lead. It was a public poem, or a poem on a public theme that sought to find images for the yearning that might have been experienced by Irish emigrants—missing home, the efforts to connect. But the poem offered no easy, consoling images. Those who left did not connect with Ireland again. Instead, "we," those who stayed in Ireland, have to admit "what we did so as not to hear them."

This dark realization in Eavan's poem was almost the opposite to the sort of hopeful rhetoric Mary Robinson had used in her campaign. History had happened, the poem suggested; nothing could be done about it except find a lens through which we might see the damage that had been done.

Thus, the poet and the politician could work together and one could inspire the other. But in time, each would have to go their own way.

I came back to Stanford in 2008 as Barack Obama's first campaign to be president of the United States took over our imagination.

As I watched Obama speak of the audacity of hope, refining his message and his appeal, I noticed that he seemed to connect more and more with elements in the life and work of James Baldwin. His story seemed to match Baldwin's, and so too his tone, just as Mary Robinson's had with Eavan Boland's.

I wrote a piece then that tried to show how much Obama, in fact, had in common with Baldwin.

Both Baldwin and Obama experienced the church and intense religious feeling as key elements in their lives. Baldwin's essay "Down at the Cross" sought to let White America into the secret that was Sunday for the Black community. "The church was very exciting. It took a long time for me to disengage myself from this excitement, and on the blindest, most visceral level, I really never have, and never will."

In *Dreams from My Father*, Barack Obama described finding religion in Chicago, hearing about the history of the Black church in America "where on bright, hot Sunday mornings all the quiet terror and open wounds of the week drained away in tears and shouts of gratitude, the clapping, waving, fanning hands reddening the embers of those same stubborn ideas—survival, and freedom, and hope."

Also, both Baldwin and Obama would discover their own Americanness outside America, Baldwin in France, the home of some of his literary ancestors, Obama in Kenya, the home of his father. There is a peculiar intensity in the quality of their connection with these foreign countries.

Baldwin moved to Paris in November 1948 when he was twenty-four. "I left America," he wrote in 1959, "because I doubted my ability to survive the fury of the color problem here . . . I wanted to prevent myself from becoming *merely* a Negro; or even merely a Negro writer."

In one of the essays in *Nobody Knows My Name*, he described attending the Conference of Negro-African Writers and Artists in Paris in 1956, finding a gap between himself and the writers who had come from Africa, suggesting an optimism about

American freedom that would not survive his experience of America over the next decade: "For what, at bottom, distinguished the Americans from the Negroes who surrounded us, men from Nigeria, Senegal, Barbados, Martinique . . . was the banal and quite overwhelming fact that we had been born in a society, which, in a way quite inconceivable for Africans, and no longer real for Europeans, was open, and in a sense which has nothing to do with justice or injustice, was free. It was a society, in short, in which nothing was fixed and we had therefore been born to a greater number of possibilities, wretched as these possibilities seemed at the instant of our birth. Moreover, the land of our forefathers' exile had been made, by that travail, our home."

Baldwin summed up the result of his experience in France: "I found myself, willy-nilly, alchemized into an American the moment I touched French soil."

In his autobiography, as Obama attempted to make sense of his Kenyan heritage, there was a serious attempt to resolve the most complex matters of identity and selfhood. Despite his best efforts to reconcile his own life at home with that of his Kenyan father, the chapters about Kenya in *Dreams from My Father* show Obama puzzled and ill at ease. Later, in his book *The Audacity of Hope*, he describes his wife Michelle's admission on a flight back from Kenya to Chicago that "she was looking forward to getting home. 'I never realized just how American I was,' she said. She hadn't realized just how free she was—or how much she cherished that freedom."

But Obama still needed to create a narrative of connection, discovery, inclusion. There is a moment when he sat by the graves of his ancestors and wept. "When my tears were finally spent, I felt a calmness wash over me. I felt the circle finally close . . . I saw that my life in America—the black life, the white life, the sense of abandonment I'd felt as a boy, the frustration and hope I'd witnessed in Chicago—all of it was connected with this small plot of earth an ocean away, connected by more than an accident of name or the color of my skin. The pain I felt was my father's pain. My questions were my brothers' questions. Their struggle, my birthright."

Those last three sentences display the great difference between Baldwin's sensibility and that of Obama, between Baldwin's fearless self-interrogating and Obama's readiness to use language that would console. Whereas Baldwin sought to make distinctions, Obama wanted to make connections. Whereas Baldwin wanted to investigate untidy truths, Obama was slowly becoming a politician.

Baldwin as a novelist could feel free in his image-making to explore areas of greater complexity than any politician can, including the most eloquent. Baldwin's essays and articles come first from the self, from the body and the beating heart, from what the eyes see and the spirit feels, and then, in a set of darting shifts in perspective, Baldwin could make his own life, his own experience, become political, public.

Although Baldwin wrote that his revenge "would be to achieve a power which outlasts kingdoms," he took an abiding interest in the worldly kingdom known as the United States of America. What, then, would he have written had he lived long enough to witness Obama's first campaign? How would he have responded to the crowds who chanted "Yes We Can!"?

Reading Baldwin's essays and journalism, it is easy to guess how he might have responded to some events, events indeed that might not have surprised him. In 1979 he wrote: "If they couldn't deal with my father, how are they going to deal with the people in the streets of Tehran? I could have told them, if they had asked."

It would be possible to add Baghdad or Basra or Kabul or Kandahar to that sentence now. In 1964 he wrote: "People who do not know who they are privately, accept, as we have accepted for nearly fifteen years, the fantastic disaster which we call American politics and which we call American foreign policy, and the incoherence of the one is an exact reflection of the incoherence of the other."

There seems only one fresh hell that happened in his country that Baldwin did not foresee. And this is the vast and merciless increase in the prison population. Baldwin saw the context for it, however, and made his own position clear in a 1964 *Playboy* article: "The failure on our part to accept the reality of pain, or anguish, of ambiguity, of death, has turned us into a very peculiar and monstrous people. It means, for one thing, and it's very serious, that people who have had no experience have no compassion. People who have had no experience suppose that if a man is a thief, he is a thief; but, in fact, that isn't the most important thing about him. The most important thing about him is that he is a man and, furthermore, that if he's a thief or a murderer or whatever he is, *you* could also be and you would know this, anyone would know this who had really dared to live."

Baldwin did not see the full implications of this, and so in the same year he wrote something that seems naïve now, perhaps the only truly naïve observation he ever made: "There is a limit to the number of people any government can put in prison, and a rigid limit indeed to the practicality of such a course." And fifteen years later, in the *Los Angeles Times*, he ended an article on a note of pure optimism: "But black people hold the trump. When you try to slaughter people, you create a people with nothing to lose. And if I have nothing to lose, what are you going to do to me? In truth, we have one thing to lose—our children. Yet we have never lost them, and there is no reason for us to do it now. We hold the trump. I say it: Patience and shuffle the cards."

The cards were shuffled all right. Indeed, the word "trump" took on a new meaning. And the idea that there was a limit to the number of people any government can put in prison became a joker.

The new rules of the game included "three strikes and you're out," with all the mindlessness, mercilessness, and lack of compassion that that implied. At the end of 2005, the year Barack Obama was sworn in as a senator, there were close to 2.2 million prisoners in federal, state, or local jails in the United States. Three thousand one hundred and forty-five Black men out of every 100,000 lived as sentenced prisoners, compared to 471 White male sentenced prisoners per 100,000 White males; this compared to an estimated 3,000 out of every 100,000 members of the population of Russia who were in jail during Stalin's reign.

Paris, Harlem

In 1972, Lionel Trilling, who had published a book on E. M. Forster three decades earlier, wrote to the novelist Cynthia Ozick that "it wasn't until I had finished my book on Forster that I came to the explicit realization that he was homosexual. I'm not sure whether this was because of a particular obtuseness on my part or because . . . homosexuality hadn't yet formulated itself as an issue in the culture."

It is a tribute to Forster's skill at creating masks and smoke screens that Trilling did not realize that the drama in Forster's novels operated partly as metaphors and systems of disguise, that the energy and tension in Forster's fiction were nourished by his secret sexuality.

Forster was one of those English men who found freedom, inspiration, and relief in places such as India and Egypt. His first great love was with a young and "profoundly handsome" Indian man whom he met in England when he was twenty-seven and later traveled to India to see. And it was in Alexandria during the First World War that Foster met one of the two men who was to mean most to him in his life and with whom he conducted a passionate affair.

Forster wrote to a friend about Mohammed el Adl, a young Egyptian tram conductor: "I have plunged into an anxious but very beautiful affair. It seemed to me—and I proved right—that something precious was being offered me and that I was offering something that might be thought precious . . . I should have been right to take the plunge, because if you pass life by it's jolly well going to pass *you* by in the future."

The second great love of Forster's life was the English policeman Bob Buckingham, whom he met in 1930; the affair continued, perhaps even intensified, after Buckingham's marriage. Wendy Moffat, in her biography of the novelist, writes about Forster's relationship to May, Buckingham's wife: "Between them Morgan [Forster] and May deftly carved out an intimate space for their respective 'marriages' to their beloved Bob." May Buckingham looked after Forster with great tenderness as he was dying.

While Forster in his personal life was open and passionate, as a public figure he remained what Moffat calls "a connoisseur of caution." In 1912, when he had written his novel *Howard's End*, he made a visit to Edward Carpenter, who was a socialist and a believer in all kinds of freedom, including sexual freedom. Carpenter lived with his boyfriend George Merrill who, one day, touched the visiting Forster "just above the buttocks." It seemed, Forster wrote, that Merrill did this to all the men he met.

The touch was electrifying. Almost fifty years later, Forster recalled the thrill: "It was as much psychological as physical. It seemed to go straight through the small of my back into my ideas without involving my thoughts."

Forster went to Harrowgate, where his mother was taking a cure, and immediately began to write a new novel, *Maurice*. It was the first time he would deal openly with homosexuality.

The fate of his book gives us an idea of how difficult it was, even for a man as admired as Forster, to deal with homosexuality openly in a novel. Forster finished the book in 1914, but he did not feel that he could publish it in his lifetime. While he did show it to some friends over the years, including Lytton Strachey and Christopher Isherwood, he believed that it could not appear "until my death and England's," as he wrote to a friend.

But Forster had a second problem. Did he have a duty not to give his homosexual protagonists a tragic ending? If he had a homosexual man committing suicide or going to prison, then would his novel not serve only to reinforce the idea that homosexuals were doomed?

"A happy ending," Forster wrote, "was imperative. I shouldn't have bothered to write otherwise. I was determined that in fiction anyway two men should fall in love and remain in it for the ever and ever that fiction allows, and in this sense Maurice and Alec [two men in *Maurice*] still roam the greenwood . . . If it ended unhappily, with a lad dangling from a noose or with a suicide pact, all would be well . . . but the lovers get away unpunished and consequently recommend crime."

Forster died in 1970; *Maurice* was published the following year.

James Baldwin's second novel *Giovanni's Room,* published in 1956, was, like Forster's *Maurice,* written in a time when homosexuality was not merely forbidden or disapproved of, but also strangely invisible. Even in his own essays, Baldwin does not fully address the matter of his own homosexuality until "Freaks and the American Idea of Manhood," published in *Playboy* in 1985, two years before his death.

It came as a surprise to Baldwin's editors that the novel's characters were all White. "I certainly could not possibly have—not at that point in my life—," Baldwin said, "handled the other great weight, the 'Negro problem.' The sexual-moral light was a hard thing to deal with. I could not handle both propositions in the same book. There was no room for it."

However, his American publisher, Knopf, wanted another novel about Harlem life. They told him that he "was a 'Negro writer' and that I reached a certain audience. They told me that I could not afford to alienate that audience, and my new book would ruin my career because I was not writing about the same things and in the same manner as I had before. They said they wouldn't publish the book as a favor to me."

The book was published in 1956 by the Dial Press in the US and Michael Joseph in the UK.

Baldwin's first dramatization of homosexuality occurs in his story "The Outing," published in 1951, in which members of a church go on an outing by boat up the Hudson River. The story concentrates on three adolescent boys who are part of the group—Johnnie and his half-brother Roy and their friend David. While David and Roy, as young teenagers, take an interest in Sylvia, one of the girls on the trip, Johnnie does not. His main interest is David.

Leaning over the railings on the topmost deck of the boat, Johnnie "looked at David's face against the sky. He shivered suddenly in the sharp, cold air and buried his face in David's shoulder. David looked down at him and tightened his hold.

"'Who do you love?' he whispered. 'Who's your boy?'

"'You,' he muttered fiercely. 'I love you.'"

The implications of this short scene are all the more powerful because they are not spelled out, or discussed by either of the characters.

Later in the story, Johnnie grows uneasy as David pays attention to Sylvia. He feels "for that moment, such a depth of love, such nameless and terrible joy and pain, that he might have fallen, in the face of that company, weeping at David's feet."

The power of the story comes from the idea that this "outing" is the high moment, the last and sharpest moment, in the relationship between Johnnie and David, although neither of them knows this. David, it is clear from the way he engages with Sylvia, will survive. Johnnie, in the story's aftermath, will be alone in dealing with the consequences of his own desire. The story ends: "After a moment Johnnie moved and put his head on David's shoulder. David put his arms around him. But now where there had been peace there was only panic and where there had been safety, danger, like a flower, opened."

The question then was, for the novelist, what to do with this danger, this panic? In "The Outing," Baldwin limited the drama to a single day for two teenagers whose interior lives are explored by suggestion. Nothing in the story has to be moved towards resolution.

How could an adult Johnnie become a protagonist in a novel in which his sexuality would be fully apparent, at least to the reader? How would he live? What would love be like for him? What would he most fear? How would danger and panic identify themselves? What would the ending of such a novel be like?

James Baldwin ends *Go Tell It on the Mountain* when John Grimes, his protagonist, is still a teenager. We are left to imagine John's life. How would such a figure grow into manhood in 1950s Harlem? How would Baldwin be able to give him freedom and complexity? And what if his homosexuality had to be dramatized, as well as his life as a profoundly sensitive and somewhat introspective African American man?

It might be easy to write about doom, as Forster was aware, but how could the search for happiness be described? Or how could a fictional space be found in which John Grimes, or a figure like him, could face his destiny, or seek to control how he lived?

———

In his essay "A Question of Identity," written in 1954, James Baldwin wrote about the Paris that would inspire *Giovanni's Room*, published two years later: "For Paris is, according to its legend, a city where everyone loses his head, and his morals, lives through at least one *histoire d'amour*, ceases, quite, to arrive anywhere on time, and thumbs his nose at the Puritans—the city, in brief, where all become drunken on the fine old air of freedom."

Exploring and deconstructing this legend worked wonders for Baldwin as a novelist. In *Giovanni's Room*, he sought to ensnare love and loyalty, commitment and truth, in a net of danger and panic. Using Paris as the backdrop offered his book not only a glamour and a kind of weight, but also meant that it was part of a tradition of American novels set in Paris in which the American characters find that the freedoms available come at a price, often the price of an uncomfortable self-knowledge.

Henry James's novel *The Ambassadors*, for example, published in 1903, is set in a Paris that allows the middle-aged Lambert Strether to live as though for the first time. In the early pages, Strether, whose mission is to return a young man called Chad Newsome, who has been worrying his mother greatly by lingering in Paris, to the family fold in Massachusetts, begins himself to savor the freedoms that Paris offers. On his second day in Paris, the city "hung before him this morning, the vast bright Babylon, like some huge iridescent object, a jewel brilliant and hard, in which parts were not to be discriminated nor differences comfortably marked. It twinkled and trembled and melted together, and what seemed all surface one moment seemed all depth the next . . . Was it at all possible . . . to like Paris enough without liking it too much?"

Strether, soon after his arrival in the city, approaches the third-floor apartment where he knows Chad lives and, as he stands on the street gazing upward, he sees a young man, who is not Chad, come out on the balcony to smoke a cigarette. As their eyes lock, Strether sees that the smoker is "very young; young enough apparently to be amused at an elderly watcher, to be curious even to see what the elderly watcher would do on finding himself watched."

In the passage that follows, the very notion of watching and being watched offers the novel considerable tension. It is as though Paris itself tempts the American novel towards dramatizing such moments. Paris will, as the novel proceeds, come to beguile Strether and tempt him as much as it will eventually deceive him and let him down.

James Baldwin, in his analysis of the novel, saw Strether's failure as a failure of masculinity. "What is the moral dilemma of Lambert Strether," Baldwin asked, "if not that, at the midnight hour, he realizes that he has, somehow, failed his manhood: that the 'masculine sensibility,' as James puts it, has failed in him?"

Baldwin goes on to praise Henry James and to denigrate those who came after him, writing that it was James's perception of Strether's weak manhood "which makes [Henry James], until today, the greatest of our novelists. For the question which he raised, ricocheting it, so to speak, off the backs of his heroines, is the question which so torments us now. The question is this: How is an American to become a man? And this is precisely the same thing as asking: How is America to become a nation? By contrast with him, the giants who came to the fore between the two world wars merely lamented the necessity."

One of these giants was Ernest Hemingway. The opening chapters of Hemingway's novel *The Sun Also Rises*, published in 1926, also take place in Paris, where many expatriates enjoy the easy freedoms of the city's bars and restaurants and clubs. The novel expands considerably on what the ominous reference in *The Ambassadors* to the "terrible toughs of the American bars and banks roundabout the Opera" implies. The Hemingway book includes references to a Paris in which homosexual men move easily.

This occurs in chapter 3 when Jake, another American in Paris whose manhood is in doubt, is standing at the doorway of a dance club and sees two taxis arriving with "a crowd of young men, some in jerseys and some in their shirt-sleeves." He can see "their hands and their newly washed, wavy hair in the light from the door. The policeman standing by the door looked at me and smiled." The smile suggests that the policeman is amused by these young men whom Jake now notices "grimacing, gesturing, talking . . . Somehow they always made me angry. I know they are supposed to be amusing, and you should be tolerant, but I wanted to swing on one, any one, anything to shatter that superior, simpering composure."

———

Paris, for James Baldwin, was never neutral space or mere backdrop, nor, as Oscar Wilde said, simply where good Americans go to die. Living in the city's freedoms allowed Baldwin to consider the implications of his own search for freedom. In the essay "The Discovery of What It Means to Be an American," published in 1959, Baldwin begins by quoting Henry James directly—"It is a complex fate being an American"—and then goes on: "The principal discovery an American writer makes in Europe is just how complex this fate is. America's history, her aspirations, her peculiar triumphs, her even more peculiar defeats, and her position in the world . . . are all so profoundly and stubbornly unique that the very word 'America' remains a new, almost completely undefined and extremely controversial proper noun."

As a teenager, Baldwin already knew that the best way to imagine Harlem was to view it through the lens of Paris. Paris was, for an ambitious Black writer, the next stop, the journey there a rite of passage. One of Baldwin's French teachers at the Frederick Douglass Junior High School in Harlem was Countee Cullen (1903–1946), who had flourished as a poet and essayist and novelist during the Harlem Renaissance. Many of his teachers, Baldwin pointed out, "were survivors of the Harlem Renaissance and wanted us black students to know that we could do anything, become anything." In his book *Baldwin's Harlem*, Herb Boyd writes about the connection between Cullen and Baldwin: "they both considered themselves less than attractive, were homosexuals, were writers . . . attended the same school, and were the 'adopted sons' of fundamentalist preachers."

Cullen, who had gone back and forth between New York and Paris from 1928 to 1934, wrote a poem "To France" in which he made clear the sense of freedom that he felt there:

There might I only breathe my latest days,
With those rich accents falling on my ear
That most have made me feel that freedom's rays
Still have a shrine where they might leap and sear

In his autobiography *A Long Way from Home,* another Harlem Renaissance writer, Claude McKay (1890–1948), wrote a description of Paris in the 1920s.

"The cream of Harlem was in Paris," McKay wrote. "The *Porgy* actors had come over from London. There was an army of school teachers and nurses. There were Negro Communists going to and returning from Russia . . . And there were painters and writers and poets, of whom the most outstanding was Countee Cullen."

The Paris to which James Baldwin came in 1948, in the wake of such luminaries, offered pleasures and freedoms to African American artists and writers that were easy to name. In an unpublished 1951 essay, "I Chose Exile," Richard Wright wrote: "To live in Paris is to allow one's sensibilities to be nourished by physical beauty. To me the most startling things in Paris are its trees which are to be found, not just in rich, residential areas, but in all sections of the city. A Parisian would find it criminal to make a Park Avenue and leave, say, Spanish Harlem to rot in dirt and garbage . . . I love my adopted city. Its sunsets, its teeming boulevards, its slow and humane tempo of life have entered deeply into my heart."

"It is because I love freedom," he wrote, "and I tell you frankly that there is more freedom in one square block of Paris than there is in the entire United States of America."

Ralph Ellison took a different view when he visited Paris in the mid-1950s: "I am getting a little sick," he wrote, "of American Negroes running over for a few weeks and coming back insisting that it's paradise . . . So many of them talk and act like sulking children and all they can say about France with its great culture is that it's a place where they can walk into any restaurant and be served. It seems rather obscene to me to reduce life in such terms."

———

Some of the atmosphere in Baldwin's novel *Giovanni's Room* came from an idea of an American outside his own country as a disruptive and untrustworthy presence. Other parts of the novel, however, were inspired not by an idea, but directly by what Baldwin saw and experienced in Paris. In an interview in 1980, he spoke of using "some of the people I met. We all met in a bar, there was a blond French guy sitting at a table, he bought us drinks. And two or three days later I saw his face in the headlines of a Paris paper. He had been arrested and was later guillotined . . . I saw him in the headlines, which reminded me that I was already working on him without knowing it."

In that interview, Baldwin also stated that his book was "not so much about homosexuality, it is what happens if you are so afraid that you finally cannot love anybody."

Giovanni's Room begins in a manner that is grave, formal. The words in the opening sentences do not have the hushed tone of guilt or confession that will come later, but rather a ring of certainty, a sense of finality. The voice is not whisper-ing, but speaking as though to a large audience. The tone is theatrical. After the first sentence, "I stand at the window of this great house in the south of France as night falls, the night which is leading me to the most terrible morning of my life," it is easy to imagine the actor preparing to turn to the audience. The next sentence—"I have a drink in my hand, there is a bottle at my elbow"—reads like a stage direction. By the end of the paragraph as the actor explains about his ancestors who "conquered a continent," he is facing the audience who will know that he is White and in full possession of the text's grave cadences.

As in *Go Tell It on the Mountain*, the opening page uses the repetition of words as a hushed refrain, with a sense of the narrative as a performance, neither simple nor linear. In the very first sentence, the word "night" is repeated; in the fifth sentence, the word "face." And then in the second paragraph, more words come twice, ordinary words, such as "train," "same," "looking," "countryside." In a sentence that uses "someone" three times ("Someone will offer to share a sandwich with me, someone will offer me a sip of wine, someone will ask for a match."), we see our narrator not only remembering with a kind of vehemence but attempting to tell the story in a way that avoids the banality of mere recounting, and that seeks to elevate and underscore with an incantatory sound.

In a piece he wrote for the *New York Times Book Review* in January 1962, Baldwin dismissed Hemingway: "his reputation began to be unassailable at the very instant that his work began that decline from which it never recovered—at about the time of *For Whom the Bell Tolls*. Hindsight allows us to say that this boyish and romantic and inflated book marks Hemingway's abdication from the efforts to understand the many-sided evil that is in the world. This is exactly the same thing as saying that he somehow gave up the effort to become a great novelist."

Nevertheless, it is clear from the second page of *Giovanni's Room*, as the narrator David describes meeting his girlfriend Hella using simple words and hypnotic repetitions to evoke a time of easy and carefree pleasures, that Hemingway's shadow has been cast over the prose. Sometimes, Baldwin's version of this can seem effortless and precise, but there are other times when it masks an unease and appears less than convincing, as when David speaks of his relationship with Hella: "I thought she would be fun to have fun with."

But there are other sounds and signs in the novel, competing ones, when the narrator's voice becomes regretful, weary, rueful, wise. David is willing to judge himself, and prepared also to use these pages not merely to explain or dramatize but to expiate his sins, as much as he can, and even repent, if that is possible.

And he also speaks in sentences that are balanced and sonorous and rhythmically complete. In a bar: "There were the usual, paunchy, bespectacled gentlemen with avid, sometimes despairing eyes, the usual knife-blade lean, tight-trousered boys . . . One could never be sure, as concerns these latter, whether they were after money or blood or love."

This last sentence has some of the lovely, lazy sound of a blues song, or a slow, smoldering, exquisite jazz riff. Filled with both irony and sadness, it indicates the mixtures that will come to dictate the destruction of at least two of the characters in the novel.

Baldwin is seeking a balance between what is relaxed and what is elevated and artificial, between a voice speaking and a voice under pressure becoming eloquent and literary and performative. It matters that the prose has few obvious, colloquial American inflexions, that Giovanni and the narrator speak in a French that is not their first language, before it is translated for the purpose of the story into English. Their dialogue, like the dialogue between the narrator and his American girlfriend, has much that is artificial and evasive. And this makes the narrative, in which the narrator faces the most difficult truths and attempts to find a voice that will further intensify his sense of the wrong he had done, more like a ceremony, a stage show. This is not the simple truth as much* as the sharply dramatic truth, and it is on display.

The novel, then, is not just recounting what happened. It is creating an atmosphere in which remorse can find expression, in which the concrete fact, set down with precision, can sit easily with the numinous and the ghostly. Thus, Giovanni's first appearance can be exact: "He stood, insolent and dark and leonine, his elbow leaning on the cash register, his fingers playing with his chin, looking out at the crowd." Soon, the same figure will reappear as a ghost: "Now someone whom I had never seen before came out of the shadows towards me. It looked like a mummy or a zombie—this was the first, overwhelming impression—of something walking after it had been put to death."

In *Giovanni's Room* there is often an aura of moral urgency. David, the narrator, is not only performing for us but he is also preaching to himself; he is using his eloquent voice to let himself know who he is and what he did. The address is directed inwards, but there is a feeling too that David is almost relishing the sound he makes, his own sweet, confessional rhetoric. He is holding the audience by the force of his own honesty, his own final admission.

But the facts also need to be set out clearly, since this is a book of evidence. On the third page we learn that Giovanni, who has been found guilty of murder, is "about to perish, sometime between this night and this morning, on the guillotine." David must finish his story before then, not because he is addressing Giovanni directly but because the death of Giovanni will eradicate the need for David to speak. He will be calculating and self-protective enough to walk away.

As the narrative progresses, and David tells of a boyhood homosexual affair, the prose becomes more dense, with more adjectives and adverbs, and longer sentences. The simplicity of setting the scene has been replaced now by the more complex music of remembering, conjuring up the context in which everything began to unfold. Slowly, this music grows in fervor as it examines danger and panic: "The power and the promise and the mystery of that body made me suddenly afraid." Or: "The very bed, its sweet disorder, testified to violence."

Since the crosscurrents in this narrative between sex and love are dangerous and ensnaring and also thrilling, Baldwin remembers early love as a preacher might speak of sin or indeed extreme religious ecstasy. He writes of sex: "I feel in myself now a faint, a dreadful stirring of what so overwhelmingly stirred in me then, great thirsty heat, and trembling, and tenderness so painful I thought my heart would burst. But out of this astounding, intolerable pain came joy, we gave each other joy that night."

To hold the tension, the novel must be short. Many scenes that could have been included, such as the ordinary, domestic life that David and Giovanni shared, their daily routines as lovers, are omitted. Giovanni's room itself and the bar where he works are described, but the world outside—the great city of Paris—is not there in any rich detail. Baldwin seems most comfortable when his characters move through a city that is almost empty. "The city, Paris, which I loved so much, was absolutely silent. There seemed to be almost no one on the streets, although it was still very early in the evening."

In *Giovanni's Room*, Baldwin is not especially interested in character. Neither Hella nor Giovanni is rendered precisely. The other characters are ciphers; they do what the narrative needs them to do. David himself is all voice, all surface response. His account of his upbringing—the death of his mother, his controlling aunt, his cruel father—seems remote, lacking in texture. This lack of focus on depth of character and backstory allows the novel to fixate on large questions of innocence and guilt, the possibility that the narrator himself is beyond redemption, as though this novel's underlying music were that of a sermon.

And the very thinness of his history matches David's response to others, including both Hella and Giovanni. His lack of self-awareness allows him to do damage and then be surprised by the consequences.

When Hella comes back from Spain, David moves in with her as though Giovanni never existed. Nothing said between them will matter. It is as if their encounter is just a holding pattern, inconsequential enough to encourage us to imagine where Giovanni is and what might happen were he to appear.

When he does materialize, all is undercurrent. They meet Giovanni, as though by accident, in a bookshop. Describing how they walk out into the street, with Giovanni leading, Baldwin writes three sentences: "The bell rang viciously as Giovanni opened the door. The evening air hit us like a blaze. We started walking away from the river, towards the boulevard."

It is that third sentence that does most of the work here. It is important that it is "we" who started walking, not "I." David does not walk away from the others. His callousness involves him doing nothing much in these moments.

It must have been tempting to give David a fresh thought or add a bright, startling word in that last sentence. But he will not come alive here. Because he does not love either Giovanni or Hella, he fades even as he speaks.

Few feelings in the novel come without their opposite. In the scene when they walk away from the river, David barely feels anything, whereas, in scenes just before, his feelings dart, wildly unstable. With Giovanni, for example, "I was guilty and irritated and full of love and pain. I wanted to kick him and I wanted to take him in my arms." Later, when he goes to Giovanni's room for the last time, he confesses: "I felt nothing for Giovanni. I felt terror and pity and a rising lust." The room that has been their haven becomes, for David, "this filthy little room."

The guilty one, the man who does damage, gets to speak and control the narrative, but David also has to register how Giovanni accuses him: "You do not love anyone! You have never loved anyone, I am sure you never will!"

The accusation sounds stark and simple, but not loving anyone is a complex act, especially since David is skilled at the outward signs of love. With Giovanni and with Hella, David feels a wayward set of emotions: one of these is need, another is a kind of coldness, and a third, strangely, has the same shape as love, but it comes accompanied by a fierce resistance to the one who might be loved.

When Hella returns to Paris from Spain, David notes: "I had hoped that when I saw her something instantaneous, definitive, would have happened in me, something to make me know where I should be and where I was. But nothing happened." David, as self-aware narrator, is anxious to look at his own part in the story truthfully and probingly. And that includes facing the fact that he himself is deeply unreliable. No emotion David feels is fixed or can be trusted. He loved Hella, he writes, "as much as ever and I still did not know how much that was."

In that first meeting at her return, David's sense that "nothing happens" begins to change. "Then I took her in my arms and something happened then. I was terribly glad to see her. It really seemed, with Hella in the circle of my arms, that my arms were home and I was welcoming her back there."

This manages to give the impression of genuine emotion. But the sentence "I was terribly glad to see her" has a hollow sound, as does "It really seemed."

David's rejection of Giovanni is, on the other hand, more sudden and colder. When Giovanni loses his job, with Hella still in Spain, the two men have a chance to be closer together. "Now—now, of course, I see something very beautiful in those days, which were such torture then. I felt, then, that Giovanni was dragging me with him to the bottom of the sea." When they run out of money, David borrows from an older homosexual, Jacques. And then, as he and Giovanni sit on a terrace, David has a sudden, sharp thought: "I looked at Giovanni and thought, for a moment, how nice it would be if Jacques would take him off my hands."

And what we notice here—and this happens in many sentences in the book—is how reduced David's Americanness becomes. He often sounds as though he does not come from anywhere in particular. His voice is not direct, despite its claim to be so. He makes a neutral sound; it is often hard to place him. He avoids using an American idiom. "How nice it would be" or "I was terribly glad to see her" sound more English than American, making clear that David is an actor, a performer. The book is a formal occasion rather than a relaxed first-person narrative. We hear a voice that is as synthetic as it is avowedly honest.

Giovanni's Room, like Henry James's late novel *The Golden Bowl*, inhabits fictional space that is heavily circumscribed. There is a city—London in *The Golden Bowl*, Paris in *Giovanni's Room*—and there are a few streets and a few interiors. But the city in neither novel is evoked with any memorable care. There is one Italian at the center of both books—the Prince in *The Golden Bowl*, Giovanni in Baldwin's novel—and two or three Americans. In both novels, the Americans always have the option of going home. There are locals, some named, some not. There are characters in both novels who are presented as pure and innocent and others who are openly malicious. There are some public gatherings, but not many. There is no obvious sense of public life in either book—no newspapers, no signs of social change, no haunting history, no tensions in the street: often nothing at all in the streets.

Instead, there are intense human relations and, as though moving like an insidious army, there is a treachery that is hidden and then exposed, accompanied by charm, by beauty, perhaps by veiled good intentions.

Since *Giovanni's Room* concerns the private life, and deals with the emotional world of a few characters with no concern at all for the France in which the novel is set, or indeed the Paris in which the characters move, it is interesting to examine a novel by another African American writer in exile in Paris, set in the city in 1960 and 1961, and published in 1963. This is William Gardner Smith's novel *The Stone Face*.

Smith was born three years after James Baldwin—in 1927—in a Black working-class district of Philadelphia. In the early 1950s he moved to Paris, where he worked as a journalist for Agence France. In Paris, Smith moved in the same small world as Baldwin, befriending writers such as Chester Himes and Richard Wright.

The Stone Face is an openly public and political novel that dramatizes the life of a Black painter and journalist in Paris as he confronts the distance between the comfort and safety that Paris offers him as a Black American and what it means to be Arab or Algerian in the same city at the same time.

Like Baldwin's novel, Smith's is an "inquiry into the ambiguities of exile," as Adam Shatz writes in an introduction to the book. While Baldwin's novel deals with the inner life of a flawed protagonist, Smith's character Simeon Brown experiences Paris as a city alive with racial tensions. It is as though Baldwin's protagonist can take time to explore difficult truths about himself because he is White, whereas Simeon Brown, as a Black man in flight from violence, has no such luxury. The private life, for him, will always be subject to what is happening in the public realm.

In a story published in 1960, "This Morning, This Evening, So Soon," James Baldwin wrote about the relationship between Harriet, a White Swedish woman, and the narrator, a Black American man in Paris who considers the implications of a life shaped by history versus a life that begins by evading history or shaking it off. "For everybody's life begins on a level where races, armies and churches stop. And yet everyone's life is always shaped by races, churches, and armies; races, churches, armies menace, and have taken, many lives."

The narrator's life in the story has been shaped by his exile. "If Harriet had been born in America, it would have taken her a long time, perhaps forever, to look on me as a man like other men; if I had met her in America, I would never have been able to look on her as a woman like all other women. The habits of public rage and power would also have been our private compulsions, and would have blinded our eyes. We would never have been able to love each other."

Baldwin's narrator is alert to the difference between being a Black American in Paris in these years and being Algerian, as the conflict between France and the Algerian National Liberation Front raged between 1954 and 1962. "And there are fewer Algerians to be found on the streets of Paris now . . . The Arab cafés are closed—those dark, acrid cafés in which I used to meet with them to drink tea, to get high on hashish, to listen to the obsessive, stringed music . . . They were perfectly prepared to drive all Frenchmen into the sea, and to level the city of Paris. And I love Paris, I will always love it, it is the city which saved my life. It saved my life by allowing me to find out who I am."

In his essay "Alas, Poor Richard," published a year after "This Morning, This Evening, So Soon," Baldwin contemplated the ambiguities around the freedom won by Black American writers such as Richard Wright in Paris: "Richard was able, at last, to live in Paris exactly as he would have lived, had he been a white man, here, in America. This may seem desirable, but I wonder if it is. Richard paid the price such an illusion of safety demands." Baldwin wrote about what he saw as Wright's loss of status in the Paris in which he had settled: "The brightest faces were now turned from him, and among these faces were the faces of the Africans and the Algerians."

William Gardner Smith's *The Stone Face* looks at the ironies surrounding the welcome his protagonist receives in Paris. Simeon and another Black expatriate take two White Swedish girls to a club in Paris, where they are greeted by the manager. Then four White American men arrive. "Their drunken raucous laughter and loud voices disturbed the peaceful atmosphere of the room." When one of them asks: "Hey, you boys from the States?" Simeon's companion replies: "Man, we ain't no boys. I'm old enough to be your mother's husband."

The reader might expect a fight to break out now, with the police called, and the two Black men carted away. Instead, the French manager says to the four White Americans: "Please leave or I'll call the police. There are certain things you have to leave behind when you come to France. At least when you come to my club."

Thus, Paris is presented as a place free of the racism Simeon has known in Philadelphia. But just after the scene in the club, on their way home, Simeon and his friend witness a man being beaten up on the street by the police and taken away in a wagon. "That man was probably an Arab," his friend says, adding "There's a war on in Algeria, remember?"

Baldwin in an interview with the magazine *Essence* in 1976 spoke about these years in Paris where "you can slide because nobody is bothering you. On the other hand, if you have the sense to look around, you see what's happening to the Algerians, the Senegalese and to any nonwhite person in Europe is the same thing that's happening to you here. So you have not really escaped anything at all . . . You could see the way the police treated the Algerians. You could see why they were being thrown in jail and dropped in the river like flies."

Later in Smith's novel, Simeon takes some Algerian friends to the nightclub from which the four White Americans were ejected only to find that he and his friends are being greeted with considerable coolness by the manager and the waiter, normally so friendly. "The Frenchmen and women at nearby tables turned to stare at them; there were whispers and laughs." Eventually, the manager says to Simeon: "We don't want you back here . . . you and your friends."

Smith has been documenting, using the novel as his medium, the different ways of being an outsider in France. In the very last section of his novel, he ceases to write like a novelist seeking to create illusions, and he takes on the tone of a documentary-maker, someone who sets out the facts as clearly as possible. He charts what happened in Paris on October 1, 1961, during the demonstration against a curfew that had been imposed on Algerians: "It was a cold, damp day. The Paris police prefecture published a communiqué warning that all gatherings on the street were banned, and that the police would break up any demonstrations that were held."

Simeon witnesses the police attack on the demonstrators: "In scenes of terrible sadism, Simeon saw pregnant women clubbed in the abdomen, infants snatched from their mothers and hurled to the ground. Along the Seine, police lifted unconscious Algerians from the ground and tossed them into the river."

Baldwin's image in the 1976 interview of Algerians "dropped in the river like flies" is startling, as is the phrase "tossed them into the river" here. As Adam Shatz writes in his introduction to Smith's book, the demonstration was, in fact, "brutally suppressed; hundreds of protestors were killed, some in the street that evening, their bodies thrown into the Seine; others were beaten to death inside the police station over the next few days." Smith's account of the massacre is, Shatz points out, "the only one that exists in the fiction of the period."

For *Giovanni's Room*, Baldwin did not eschew what was happening in France politically, but he used a strategy that had animated and rescued *Go Tell It on the Mountain*: he moved the novel from secular space, a place filled with material desires, towards a religious or spiritual realm. To do this, he had to deal not with the mundane matters of most novels, but with the large question of guilt and sin and the even larger question of love as abstract and exalted and yet fatally human, small, easy to crush.

In 1964 in a letter, Lionel Trilling spotted an element he objected to in Baldwin's public rhetoric. "I find myself antagonistic to all ethics of love," Trilling wrote, "and, indeed, to the whole concept . . . of love as it exists nowadays. Nothing—for example—seems more horrible to me in the present racial situation here than James Baldwin's prescription that it be dealt with by love. My feeling is for a much colder word, 'respect.' This suggests to me all kinds of delightful possibilities, as love does not—on the contrary, indeed."

The problem in *Giovanni's Room*, however, is that David cannot love. In *Giovanni's Room*, there cannot be a happy ending because the impediments to happiness come from within. David and Giovanni control their own fates, or seem to. Baldwin sought to leave his characters free—or not openly and obviously burdened by what might restrict them—in order to see how they might live.

The room, Giovanni's room, begins as a haven and ends as a kind of airless cell. The suggestion is that David, as an American, comes to take what he wants and, bored with Giovanni, goes elsewhere, leaving havoc in his wake.

But there is another way of reading the book as a novel so profoundly about restriction that the restrictions barely need to be mentioned.

It may seem that the events of the novel happen outside

any fixed society. But there are other people in the novel: Guillaume, and Jacques, two older gay men, solitary, predatory figures; the book also includes a number of young men who need money, and some unnamed people who hang around bars. That, effectively, is the Paris of the novel.

The Stone Face, William Gardner Smith's novel, looks like a panorama beside Baldwin's tiny canvas. Yet Smith's novel, much of the time, seems arranged around a set of emotions that can easily be predicted and events that could routinely be reported in a newspaper. Simeon mostly notices and experiences as a way of satisfying a deliberately devised paradigm.

Baldwin wishes to remove a social and political context from two homosexual men not merely to isolate them and thus see their anxieties more clearly, but also to dramatize the idea that the love between these two men requires a context, a hinterland, in which to thrive. It cannot happen for long in a small room. Their love needs a city. And there is no city, or not much of one. Instead, there is repression, depicted as if this were something natural. And, thus, in Giovanni's room where they come for shelter, they find that they are trapped.

———

It might be hard, for readers now, to imagine a moment when gay life in cities was both deeply secretive and oddly on display. It might seem that *Giovanni's Room* is set in the dark, distant past. But when I went to live in Barcelona in 1975, just twenty years after Baldwin's novel had been published, there were no gay bars in the city. Instead, there were a few bars that were rumored to be gay-friendly. People hung out there, often men alone. Sometimes, it was hard to know what they were looking for. At other times, in a bar like Café de la Opera or El Drugstore beside the opera house, everyone was just watching. But there was nothing to watch.

The streets nearby were different. Gay men moved among the crowds once darkness fell as if they were going somewhere. If you sat at the window of a bar you could see the same man doubling back on the street and appearing again. After the dictator Francisco Franco died in November 1975, the change came only gradually. I remember hearing a rumor of an actual gay bar, but I never found it. Instead, life on the streets grew more intense. On some side streets—Carrer dels Escudellers, for example—it was easy to see that most men were quietly and seriously gay and were busily hunting for sex.

A few times in that first year in the city, I met a guy I liked and wanted to meet again. Once, I regretted that I had not got a phone number from a fellow I had gone home with; I was sorry that I had not made some arrangement to see him again. He stayed in my mind. I imagined, as the weather got better, what it might be like to go to the beach with him. All I had was a memory of one night in bed with him.

And then one Saturday evening on the Ramblas—the long boulevard in Barcelona—I saw him coming towards me. For one second, maybe two, I felt that this was going to matter. Clearly, he saw me as we approached each other. We were both alone. I, for one, was going nowhere. He nodded politely and knowingly as he passed by. He saw no reason why he should stop. He wasn't afraid of anything. It was just that we had had sex once. Like most people then, he saw no reason why we should bother sleeping together a second time.

In that same season, I was in a cheap restaurant one night with a friend. We had to share a table with a guy who was on his own. We were talking in English; he could not understand us. He watched us, smiled a few times. I began to glance at him. When my friend went to the bar or the bathroom, this stranger turned to me and in slow, careful Spanish—so I would understand—he asked if my friend and I were partners. When I said no, he asked if he and I could have a drink together after dinner.

Later, when it came to be closing time in another bar, he wanted to know if, instead of having sex tonight, I might meet him another time and, since we were both single in the city, if I might think of seeing him a few times more. We huddled in a doorway and kissed. He was serious. He really did want to have sex now, he said, but he believed it would be better if we waited and met again a day or two later.

We must have spoken about sex, types of sex, because he used a phrase that I never heard in ordinary speech in Spanish before or since. When he wanted to say *to fuck*, instead of using a verb such as *follar*, he used a very formal phrase, like something from Latin. He said *penetrar el recto*. He gave me a phone number where I might find him.

I made no decision not to call him. I let days pass. But I did not phone him and I never saw him again. Such encounters, promising and then nothing much, seemed part of the deal in those years in Barcelona.

In this modern European city, where homosexuals were

plenty but images of gay life were scarce, where much was fleeting and furtive, it would be easy to imagine that something had atrophied in all of us, that we were, like David in Baldwin's book, eager to *penetrar el recto* but unable to love. But that idea dissolved as the city changed. As Barcelona became a gay metropolis, no one gay felt we couldn't love. The problem had not been the lovers, we learned, or the rooms we were in; the problem was the silence, the invisibility, the strangeness.

═════

James Baldwin took this idea for granted as he turned his gaze in *Giovanni's Room* not on the city but on the soul. He saw the dramatic possibilities of two men locked in a dream in a room in a time when gay people had no easy place in the world. *Giovanni's Room* was, however, not a plea for understanding, or for social change. Rather, it was a cry from the depths.

The confessional, self-lacerating style of the narrative, filled with sudden flourishes and painful realizations, has something in common with another text, another cry from the depths, where the narrator, also writing in a dark time, has also been wounded and has caused pain, and the motives are also gnarled and require careful explanation and emotional shifts of gear.

In this other text, one man is also in prison, the other, his former lover, ostensibly free. The two men, like David and Giovanni, come from different countries. One of them has a close involvement with a woman, as David does with Hella. One of them has a difficult father, as David does. And one of them sets out to write down what happened using a style that is relentless in its efforts to accuse and self-accuse, a style that is both intimate and public, using repetition of phrases and single words, using well-balanced sentences, attempting to move what was often tawdry and miserable into a spare, shimmering space where the truth might be told and redemption might almost be won.

Oscar Wilde's *De Profundis* was written under strange circumstances. In 1895, Wilde was sentenced to two years hard labor under the Victorian laws against homosexuality. In prison, he was not allowed to write. Indeed, he was hardly allowed to read. The writing of the letter (later published posthumously as the book entitled *De Profundis*) during the final months of Wilde's sentence was only possible because of the gradual relaxation in the severity of the prison regime. Under the new rules, Wilde was to be allowed pen and paper, and while what he wrote was removed each evening, it was handed back to him in the morning. Because *De Profundis* was in the form of a long letter, it would then be his property when he left the prison.

By the time Wilde began, his love for Lord Alfred Douglas, to whom the letter is addressed, had turned from fierce attachment into bitterness. As with *Giovanni's Room*, there is often a beautiful, calm eloquence in the writing. There is also a sense of urgency, of matters newly realized being said because there might not be time or opportunity to say them in the future.

The style is fluent and sweeping, with carefully controlled emotional cadence and measured elegance. The change in Wilde's voice from the voice he'd used in his plays and his fiction is astonishing, with a new range and depth and a new attention to feeling, and yet with the old skills and tricks in pitch and paradox still in place.

The letter cannot be read for its accurate account of the relationship between Wilde and his lover. That is not the point. Nor can it be read, as Wilde's poems can be read, as an effort at the creation of a purely beautiful music. *De Profundis* has neither the informality of a personal letter nor the art of a piece of imaginative writing. Its seductive, hurt, and passionate tone places it in a different category. Wilde is desperately wounded, but he is still in command of his sentences. In the dim light of the prison cell and with his suffering fresh, it was as though he sought a new sort of tension between breathlessness and breath control in his writing.

De Profundis, despite everything, is a sort of love letter, even though it might not have been meant like that nor indeed been greatly welcomed by its ostensible recipient at the time.

It is unlikely that James Baldwin ever read *De Profundis*; there is no suggestion that he was influenced by it. Wilde's text, however, throws light on why *Giovanni's Room* remains so powerful. Both books dramatize the love between two men under pressure. Both use confession as a form in a time when so much about homosexuality was kept in the dark. Both texts use searing intensity: self-awareness and self-knowledge are forced onto the page as if after a struggle; something is being said for the very first time.

In both works, the writer is concerned with who is at fault. In general, Wilde blames Douglas, while David in *Giovanni's Room* blames himself. It is as though passion unraveled because of weakness and bad faith. Both narrators—Wilde, and the David of Baldwin's novel—make it personal, and they write as though homosexual men controlled their own fate.

But the tension in their stories comes from the hidden, insidious, almost unmentionable knowledge that this idea of blame and responsibility is an illusion. It merely seemed that they controlled their own fate. Wilde and David were, in fact, helpless.

And for not knowing that they could not escape their fates, for hoping, with E. M. Forster, for a happy ending, they pay a price. We learn at the very beginning of Wilde's letter what has happened: his address is Reading Gaol. And we learn on the third page of *Giovanni's Room* that this is the last night of Giovanni's life; he will "perish" on the guillotine in the morning.

In each book, a man is to be sacrificed. In each book, the sacrifice is delineated in a manner stylized to approach parable, as an outcome that was inevitable but did not seem so to the men involved. In the end, their innocence appears also to be holy. Wilde in *De Profundis* will compare himself to Christ in his suffering; David in *Giovanni's Room* will say "that Judas and the Savior had met in me."

Baldwin, in this novel, made clear that he could work wonders with the light and shade of intimacy; that he could move easily and effortlessly into a whispered prose, in moments where David is frightened into sharp wisdom, and then with equal facility he could evoke the excitement of a crowded bar, filled with sexual expectation.

The tone continues to shift back and forth, from pure eloquence to soaring sequences to simple description. As David and Giovanni meet, Baldwin allows in the shadow of Hemingway once more: "I watched him as he moved. And then I watched their faces watching him. And then I was afraid. I knew that they were watching, had been watching both of us. They knew they had witnessed a beginning and now they would not cease to watch until they saw the end. It had taken some time but the tables had been turned, now I was in the zoo, and they were watching."

But he can follow this soon after with passages that have a gorgeous, fearless sound, pure Baldwin, tempered by dark knowledge and pain, such as when, at the end of chapter 2, the memory of Giovanni is evoked: "Until I die there will be those moments, moments seeming to rise up out of the ground like Macbeth's witches, when his face will come before me, that face in all its changes, when the exact timbre of his voice and tricks of his speech will nearly burst my ears, when his smell will overpower my nostrils. Some times, in the days which are coming—God grant me the grace to live them: in the glare of the grey morning, sour-mouthed, eyelids raw and red, hair tangled and damp from my stormy sleep, facing, over coffee and cigarette smoke, last night's impenetrable, meaningless boy who will shortly rise and vanish like the smoke, I will see Giovanni again, as he was that night, so vivid, so winning, all of the light of that gloomy tunnel trapped around his head."

The switches in the novel's style are matched by changes in perspective. For example, we are led to see the older men in the book are venal, somehow beneath contempt, as they hunt for love or sex like tired old animals. And then in chapter 3,

David has a conversation with his friend Jacques, an older homosexual man, in which he tells him that "a lot of your life *is* despicable." Jacques replies: "I could say the same about yours. There are so many ways of being despicable it quite makes one's head spin. But the way to be really despicable is to be contemptuous of other people's pain. You ought to have some apprehension that the man you see before you was once even younger than you are now and arrived at his present wretchedness by imperceptible degrees."

Swiftly, the moral center turns, and is now held by the older man. Baldwin then goes back to the central moment in Henry James's novel *The Ambassadors*, when Strether, the older man, finds himself in conversation in Paris with a younger man, also an American. In one of the most famous passages in all of James's work, Strether tells his companion: "Live all you can; it's a mistake not to. It doesn't so much matter what you do in particular so long as you have your life." Now, Jacques, in discussing David's relationship with Giovanni, tells David: "Love him, love him and let him love you. Do you think anything else under heaven really matters?"

Gradually, the simple story of love fills with ambiguity and inconstancy. If in one moment David feels deep love for Giovanni, then he will see another boy, a stranger, and feel the same for him. And then as the warmth of love becomes entangled with faithlessness, it moves even further away from love. "I felt sorrow and shame and panic and great bitterness." This will be followed within a few sentences by "There opened in me a hatred for Giovanni which was as powerful as my love and was nourished by the same roots."

No feeling is stable in this novel that attempts by a set of opposing images to find a place where something finally can be said which is true, even if it is too late. This effort to reach a healing dialectic, however, is futile; despite its intensity, it will make no difference. Later, as the story comes to an end, David will confess his immense confusion. Like Strether in *The Ambassadors*, and Jake in *The Sun Also Rises*, the narrator of *Giovanni's Room* will suffer from feelings of inadequacy, thus increasing his outsider status but adding to his ability to observe others more sharply.

The people whom David meets also live in a state of radical contradictions, including the girl with whom he sleeps who, as they are parting, "wore the strangest smile I have ever seen. It was pained, vindictive and humiliated but she inexpertly smeared across this grimace a bright girlish gaiety—as rigid as the skeleton beneath her flabby body."

Just as in *The Ambassadors*, in *Giovanni's Room* there is a parent in America who wants David to come "home," at a time when the very idea of home for him is becoming increasingly fraught with ironies. In the second part of the book David sees a sailor on the street who made him "think of home—perhaps home is not a place but simply an irrevocable condition."

But the sailor also, as they pass, brings home to him another "home." This is the home of his sexuality, which is both hidden and apparent. "We came abreast and, as though he had seen some all-revealing panic in my eyes, he gave me a look contemptuously lewd and knowing."

The sailor sees David's secret as much as he has seen David.

Concealment and disclosure are central to *Giovanni's Room*, as the narrator moves from being or seeming straight to being or seeming homosexual to being or seeming to be both, all the time prepared and unprepared to reveal himself or his confusion by a look, a stare, a moment of pure recognition.

A writer of fiction can create a double, someone who shadows the writer in some ways and varies from the writer in others. The characters we imagine move in and out of our emotional orbit, becoming versions of our secret selves, disguised aspects of our dream-otherness. While Robert Louis Stevenson created Dr. Jekyll and Mr. Hyde, Oscar Wilde created Dorian Gray, Henry James created his divided figures in "The Private Life" and "The Jolly Corner," Joseph Conrad created his doubled characters in "The Secret Sharer," every novelist, by creating a character at all, makes someone whom only the novelist might fully and vividly recognize, an emerging self that lives within the self, passing for real, passing for fictional, wavering and hovering in the dream-space between the two. A novelist can create a self-portrait; a woman novelist can make a man; a contemporary novelist can make a figure from the past; an Irish novelist can make a German; a straight novelist can make a homosexual; an African American novelist can make a White American.

Novelists slowly refashion themselves and, as a result, characters emerge on the page and then in the reader's imagination as though nothing untoward had, in fact, occurred. It is called freedom, or what James Baldwin, in another context, called "the common history—ours."

What begins to happen in *Giovanni's Room* is that David starts to notice ambiguous responses, divided emotions, not only in himself but in others. When Hella returns from Spain, for example, he sees: "Her smile was at once bright and melancholy." And he knows: "Everything was as it had been between us and at the same time everything was different." Giovanni, as the book nears its end, also begins to appear divided in his responses, thus becoming a more substantial, and more nuanced, presence. In the scene where Giovanni says that David does not love anyone, for example, Giovanni "grasped me by the collar, wrestling and caressing at once, fluid and iron at once." Soon, as they are ready to part, Giovanni is allowed to be the one with the complex set of responses: "I saw that he was shaking—with rage, or pain, or both." Later, as he imagines Giovanni with Guillaume, his old employer whom he will murder, David allows him a gnarled response: "The smile with which he responds to Guillaume almost causes him to vomit."

In the last pages of the book, the style reverts to the earlier simplicity. Sentences of stark dispassion take on a greater power after the complex, intensified colors that Baldwin has used in both the passages of description and the passages of reflection and analysis. The possibility of a rich, ambiguous, fervid response to love—or the chance of love—is over. Now, the diction needs clear statements, with full stops. "She began to cry. I held her in my arms. I felt nothing at all."

Towards the end, Hella, in confronting David, makes a point that would not have been lost on Henry James, who specialized in writing about Americans who come to no good in Europe, and indeed would have been recognized by the Hemingway of

The Sun Also Rises, a book in which Americans create chaos as they wander in Europe. Hella says: "Americans should never come to Europe, it means they can never be happy again. What's the good of an American who isn't happy? Happiness was all we had."

The Private Life

In his review of James Baldwin's third novel, *Another Country,* Lionel Trilling asked: "How, in the extravagant publicness in which Mr. Baldwin lives, is he to find the inwardness which we take to be the condition of truth in the writer?"

But Baldwin's sense of inwardness had been nourished as much as it had been damaged by the excitement and danger that came from what was public and urgent. *Go Tell It on the Mountain* and *Giovanni's Room* dramatized the conflict between a longing for a private life, even a spiritual life, and the ways in which history and politics intrude most insidiously into the very rooms we try hardest to shut them out of.

Baldwin had, early in his career, elements of what T. S. Eliot attributed to Henry James, "a mind so fine that it could not be penetrated by an idea." The rest of the time, however, he did not have this luxury, as public events pressed in on his imagination.

Baldwin's imagination remained passionately connected to the destiny of his country. He lacked the guile and watchfulness that might have tempted him to keep clear of what was happening in America; the ruthlessness he had displayed in going to live in Paris and publishing *Giovanni's Room* was no use to him later as the battle for civil rights grew more fraught. It was inevitable that someone with Baldwin's curiosity and moral seriousness would want to become involved; and inevitable that someone with his sensitivity and temperament would find what was happening all-absorbing.

Baldwin's influence arose from his books and his speeches, and from the tone he developed in essays and television appearances, a tone that took its bearings from his own experience in the pulpit. Instead of demanding reform or legislation, Baldwin grew more interested in the soul's dark, intimate spaces and the importance of the personal and the private.

In 1959, in reply to a question about whether the 1950s as a decade "makes special demands on you as a writer," Baldwin adopted his best style, lofty and idealistic and candid, while remaining sharp, direct, and challenging: "But finally for me the difficulty is to remain in touch with the private life. The private life, his own and that of others, is the writer's subject— his key and ours to his achievement."

Baldwin was interested in the hidden and dramatic areas in his own being, and was prepared as a writer to explore difficult truths about his own private life. In his fiction, he had to battle for the right of his protagonists to choose or influence their destinies. He knew about guilt and rage and bitter privacies in a way that few of his White novelist contemporaries did. And this was not simply because he was Black and homosexual; the difference arose from the very nature of his talent, from the texture of his sensibility. "All art," he wrote, "is a kind of confession, more or less oblique. All artists, if they are to survive, are forced, at last, to tell the whole story, to vomit the anguish up."

Baldwin understood the singular importance of the novel, because he saw the dilemma his country faced as essentially an interior one, as his fellow citizens suffered from a poison that began in the individual spirit and then made its way into politics. And his political writing remains as intense and vivid as his fiction, because he believed that social reform could not occur through legislation alone but required a reimagining of the private realm. Thus, for Baldwin, an examination of the individual soul as dramatized in fiction had immense power.

Baldwin's reputation as a novelist and essayist rests mainly on the work he did in the decade before 1963, a decade in which he was passionately industrious. The year 1963 seems to have been a watershed for him. He wrote hardly any fiction in that year. It was a time in which "the condition of truth" could not be achieved by solitude or by silence or by slow work on a novel.

Baldwin began the year by going on a lecture tour for the Congress of Racial Equality, known as CORE. In the first few days of January, he met James Meredith, the first Black student to enroll at the University of Mississippi despite being denied admission by the state's governor. Meredith noted how quiet Baldwin was, but he was also amused by Baldwin's version of the dance known as the twist.

Also in January of 1963, Baldwin met Medgar Evers. They

began to travel together in Mississippi, investigating the murder of a Black man and visiting the sort of churches that Baldwin's stepfather, model for the Gabriel of *Go Tell It on the Mountain*, would have preached in.

When Baldwin returned to New York, where he lived in a two-room walkup on West 18th Street, he became involved, with Lorraine Hansberry and others, in various protests. He also had a busy social life. His biographer David Leeming writes: "He still had the 'poor boy's' fascination with the rich and famous and they were just as fascinated by him. He found it difficult to refuse their frequent invitations. In short, the work was not getting done."

In the spring of 1963, to find peace, Baldwin travelled to Turkey, which had become one of his havens.

In May 1963, back in the US, Baldwin spoke in nine cities on the west coast over ten days, earning around five hundred dollars a speech, all of which went to CORE. In that month, his face appeared on the cover of the mainstream magazine *Time*. Three days later, when a friend gave a party for him at a restaurant in Haight-Ashbury, "literally hundreds of people struggled at the window to get a glimpse of him," David Leeming reports.

Two days later, Baldwin was in Connecticut, and then with two hours' sleep, he went to New York for a meeting with Attorney General Robert Kennedy.

On May 12, Baldwin had wired Kennedy blaming the federal government for failing to protect nonviolent protestors who had been beaten by police in Birmingham, Alabama. Now, on May 24, Baldwin and other activists, including Lorraine

Hansberry, Lena Horne, and Harry Belafonte, met Robert Kennedy at his home. It is not clear what Kennedy wanted from the meeting. If Kennedy's tone was patronizing, Baldwin's was not conciliatory. "They wanted something from the Kennedys that went beyond civil rights law," David Leeming writes. "They wanted the president, for instance, to escort a black child into a Deep South school. Kennedy rejected this as a 'meaningless moral gesture.'"

The most contentious moment came when a young activist who had been beaten by police told Kennedy that he could not conceive of fighting for his country. And this seemed to shock Kennedy, who claimed that as a descendant of Irish immigrants he too knew about discrimination. Lorraine Hansberry, incensed, walked out of the meeting. Baldwin later said: "I've only met one person Lorraine could not get through to, and that was the late Bobby Kennedy."

The meeting went nowhere. Its main result was to increase the FBI's interest in Baldwin.

In this same year—1963—as Baldwin made speeches, attended meetings, and stayed up late, he had many plans for work, including a book on the FBI. James Campbell writes in his biography: "Baldwin never produced his threatened work on the FBI, but he had, as usual, a multitude of other plans in mind, including the slave novel—now entitled *Tomorrow Brought Us Rain*—a screen treatment of *Another Country*, a musical version of *Othello*, a play called *The 121st Day of Sodom*, which [Ingmar] Bergman intended to produce in Stockholm, and a text for a book of photographs [by] . . . Richard Avedon."

Baldwin worked on the Avedon text after the assassination

of Medgar Evers on June 12, 1963. It has all the hallmarks of his best writing: the high tone taken from the Bible, from the sermon, from Henry James, and from a set of beliefs that belonged fundamentally to Baldwin himself and gave him his signature voice: "For nothing is fixed, forever and forever, it is not fixed; the earth is always shifting, the light is always changing, the sea does not cease to grind down rock. Generations do not cease to be born, and we are responsible to them because we are the only witnesses they have."

In August, Baldwin flew some members of his family to Puerto Rico to celebrate his birthday. Then he went to Paris, where he led five hundred people in a protest to the US embassy, returning to the US in time for the March on Washington at the end of the month. In September he went to Selma to work on voter registration. The following month he went to Canada. In December, he travelled to Africa to celebrate the independence of Kenya.

When Baldwin was asked how and where he had written his play *Blues for Mr. Charlie*, he replied: "On pads in planes, trains, gas stations—all sorts of places. With a pen or a pencil . . . This is a handwritten play." It was the only writing he completed in 1963.

———

Part of James Baldwin's fame arose from his skill as a television performer. On camera, he used clear, well-made sentences. At times, he spoke like a trained orator, channeling his views into sharp wit, fresh insight, with impressive verbal command. What he displayed was an intelligence that could quickly become grounded and combative and political once the television lights were on.

In some early appearances such as one on *The Dick Cavett Show* with the Yale philosopher Paul Weiss, Baldwin's arguments were too complex for the short time he had been allotted. Because his delivery was slightly halting—he was articulate in bursts—he was too easy to interrupt, and he was always at his best when he could speak without interruption.

It was as though he was sometimes too thoughtful for television. This, of course, also gave him an edge. It meant that he was not mimicking politicians or TV regulars. He sought to challenge, and set about thinking aloud. There were moments when he loved a simple question so that the answer could be ruminative and complicated. He used a context such as a talk show to state the most difficult truths in a style that belonged to the sermon or the seminar more naturally than the television studio.

He knew how to slow down, so that the camera lingered on his face as he prepared himself to say something difficult. He had a way, when he was about to offer an opinion that might seem extreme or unpalatable to his host or his audience, to hesitate, to let the camera see him thinking, and then to return to fluency.

At times, Baldwin's manner in television interviews and in public debates could be scathing and indignant. But he could also be calm and self-possessed. In a 1963 debate in Florida, for example, even though his fellow panelists were hostile, Baldwin remained polite. He was ready to talk about the private life, the creation of the self, in a way that no one could argue with, since he himself had set the tone and the terms. He was also ready to make clear that the lives of White people, too, had been maimed by segregation. But what was most notable is how he moved his face towards the light, how he spoke with authority, and how at home he seemed to be in a television studio.

There were times when Baldwin appeared like a method actor playing out the part of thoughtfulness, working out as the camera rolled how a man considering things carefully might appear.

While he could be provocative, he was also measured. He exuded a sort of melancholy wisdom. At times, he managed to sound optimistic, especially in a panel discussion in August 1963, at the time of the March on Washington, when he was in the company of Harry Belafonte, Marlon Brando, Sidney Poitier, and Charlton Heston.

When Lionel Trilling wrote of the "extravagant publicness in which Mr. Baldwin lives" and wondered how Baldwin might find "the inwardness which we take to be the condition of truth in the writer," Trilling was still in a world where it was presumed that writers should be quiet and stay home. And Trilling was not alone in believing that Baldwin was destroying his talent by going on television, writing articles, giving speeches, and being distracted by whatever was happening on the street.

But Baldwin belongs to a group of writers, born in the 1920s and early 1930s, who wrote both fiction and essays with a similar zeal and ambition; they did not see nonfiction as a lesser form or reporting as a lesser task. It was not easy to make a judgment on whether they were mainly novelists or, more likely, essayists who happened to write fiction. Also, it was often hard to make a judgment on what constituted their best work.

For example: Norman Mailer's *Armies of the Night* and his *Miami and the Siege of Chicago*, both works of imaginative and original political reporting, may equal his best novel, *The Executioner's Song*. So, too: V. S. Naipaul's long essay on the dictatorship in Argentina, "The Return of Eva Peron," and his autobiographical essay *Finding the Center* may match in power his novels *The House of Mister Biswas* and *The Enigma of Arrival*. Joan Didion's *Slouching Towards Bethlehem* and *The White Album* may be better than her novels *A Book of Common Prayer* and *Democracy*.

These writers—Baldwin, Mailer, Naipaul, Didion—traveled, took an interest in life, and accepted commissions from editors. And all four understood that if writing is a display of personality, then their literary personality was, no matter what form they used, lavish enough to blur the distinction between reportage and high literary fiction.

But there are also times when all four of them took on too much; their interest in a subject was sometimes not equaled by their account of it. Baldwin's book on the child murders that occurred between 1979 and 1981 in Atlanta, *Evidence of Things Not Seen*, is slack and rambling; Mailer's *Advertisements for Myself* and *Marilyn: A Biography* are not quite readable now, their egotism bloated and out of control; Naipaul's travel books often present someone too mean and irascible, more interested in showing off his own crankiness than in exploring the world outside. And Joan Didion's book *Salvador* might have been helped by more research.

What is fascinating about Baldwin's occasional journalism and speechmaking is how uneven it is, and how rapidly this can give way to insights and sharp analysis and then a glorious, sweeping, seemingly effortless final set of statements and assertions.

As he worked fast on these stray pieces for magazines, Baldwin refused to settle for a simplified version of his own oppression. Instead, he combined irony and urgency in the same thought, seeking a manner that took its bearings from somewhere high above us, perhaps even from his own unique access to the word of the Lord.

"In a very real sense," he wrote, "the Negro problem has become anachronistic; we ourselves are the only problem, it is our hearts that we must search."

In "As Much Truth as One Can Bear," a *New York Times Book Review* article from January 14, 1962, when others might have been concerned about the police or about housing, Baldwin wrote about private loneliness as though it were the most pressing problem facing Americans: "The loneliness of those cities described in [the work of John] Dos Passos is greater now than it has ever been before; and these cities are more dangerous now than they were before, and their citizens are yet more unloved . . . The trouble is deeper than we wish to think: the trouble is in us."

Sometimes, in his journalism and in his speeches, Baldwin was amusing himself. He took words such as "equality" or "identity" and concepts such as Whiteness and examined them with a mixture of mischief and a sort of Swiftian contempt.

For example, in an address to Harlem teachers in October 1963, he sought to explode the myth of the original, heroic, White settlers in America: "What happened was that some people left Europe because they couldn't stay there any longer and had to go some place else to make it. That's all. They were hungry, they were poor, they were convicts. Those who were making it in England, for example, did not get on the Mayflower."

In an essay called "The White Problem," published in 1964, Baldwin sneered at the icons of White America, insisting that the difference between White and Black in the US was close to the difference between foolishness and seriousness. To make this point sharper, he poured scorn on "Doris Day and Gary Cooper: two of the most grotesque appeals to innocence the world has ever seen. And the other, subterranean, indispensable, and denied, can be summed up in the tone and face of Ray Charles. And there never has been in this country any genuine confrontation between these two levels of experience." Innocence and experience, thus, were viewed by Baldwin through the lens of race.

He sought to elevate what was complex, multifarious, intricate. In 1966, he wrote: "Much of the American confusion, if not most of it, is a direct result of the American effort to avoid dealing with the Negro as a man."

Since he had it in for easy and fixed categories, he was bound eventually to become eloquent about how his society dealt with the idea of men and masculinity.

In the early 1960s, Baldwin spoke in an interview with *Mademoiselle* magazine about sexuality in his customarily challenging tone: "American males are the only people I've ever encountered in the world who are willing to go on the needle before they go to bed with each other."

While early in his career Baldwin did not speak directly about his own sexuality, others were ready to offer hints and innuendos. A 1963 *Time* magazine profile, for example, described Baldwin as a "nervous, slight, almost fragile figure, filled with frets and fears. He is effeminate in manner, drinks considerably, smokes cigarettes in chains."

When Lionel Trilling worried about Baldwin's "extravagant publicness," the implications of the word "extravagant" would not have been lost on many readers. And when Norman Mailer wrote of Baldwin that "even the best of his paragraphs are sprayed with perfume," he would not have been easily misunderstood. Also, the extensive FBI file on James Baldwin included the sentence: "It has been heard that Baldwin may be a homosexual and he appeared as if he may be one."

Baldwin, in his own writings, was often careful. He liked complex connections, strange distinctions, ambiguous implications. Thus, even in a time when gay identity was becoming easier to denote or define, Baldwin resisted the very concept of gay and straight, even male and female, insisting in an essay in 1985 that "each of us, helplessly and forever, contains the other—male in female, female in male, white in black and black in white. We are part of each other. Many of my countrymen appear to find this fact exceedingly inconvenient and even unfair, and so, very often, do I. But none of us can do anything about it."

Religious elements in the civil rights movement were suspicious of both Baldwin and Bayard Rustin, a prominent organizer and activist who was close to Martin Luther King Jr. While King was not personally bothered by Rustin's homosexuality, some of his colleagues were. One of them suggested that Baldwin and Bayard "were better qualified to lead a homosexual movement than a civil rights movement." Baldwin's homosexuality may have been one of the reasons why he was not invited to speak at the March on Washington in 1963.

But these were minor irritations compared to what happened when Baldwin's fellow activists began to absorb fully the implications not only of *Giovanni's Room* but also of *Another Country*. Baldwin's third novel, published in 1962, became a bestseller, and showed Rufus, its Black hero, as, in the words of the Black Panther leader Eldridge Cleaver, "a pathetic wretch who indulged in the white man's pastime of committing suicide, who let a white bisexual homosexual [*sic*] fuck him in the ass, and who took a Southern Jezebel for his woman."

Cleaver, in his book *Soul on Ice*, published in 1968, had no difficulty identifying the problem: "It seems that many Negro homosexuals . . . are outraged and frustrated because in their sickness they are unable to have a baby by a white man. . . . Homosexuality is a sickness, just as are baby-rape or wanting to become the head of General Motors."

Baldwin wrote about Cleaver in *No Name in the Street*: "He seemed to feel that I was a dangerously odd, badly twisted, and fragile reed, of too much use to the Establishment to be trusted by blacks . . . Well, I certainly hope I know more about myself, and the intention of my work than that, but I *am* an odd quantity. So is Eldridge; so are we all." Later, in an interview with the *Paris Review* in 1984, Baldwin said "my real difficulty with Cleaver, sadly, was visited on me by the kids who were following him, while he was calling me a faggot and the rest of it."

It would have been easy then for Baldwin to have gone into exile, disillusioned and sad, to have written his memoirs and become nostalgic about the glory days of the civil rights movement. Indeed, he was planning to write a book about the murdered leaders Medgar Evers, Malcolm X, and Martin Luther King.

But this is not what happened. As the 1960s went on, Baldwin became energized and excited by the Black Panthers, whose leaders he first met in San Francisco late in 1967. The three leaders—Huey Newton, Bobby Seale, and (despite their antipathies) Eldridge Cleaver—were, David Leeming writes, "as far as Baldwin was concerned, the future of the civil rights movement . . . Baldwin admired the radicals; he saw them as part of the larger 'project' of which the old civil rights movement had been only a stage." Baldwin wrote a preface to one of Seale's books and supported Newton when, soon after their first meeting, he was arrested and imprisoned.

He also became more militant in his television interviews. For example in an interview with Dick Cavett aired on June 16, 1969, he said: "If we were white, if we were Irish, if we were Jewish or if we were Poles, if we had in fact, in your mind, a frame of reference, our heroes would be your heroes too,

Martin would be a hero and not be a threat, Malcolm X might still be alive. You can trace in some ways the discontent of white people when they rise, they are heroes, everyone is very proud of brave little Israel, a state against which I have nothing . . . I don't want to be misinterpreted, I am not an anti-Semite. But you know, when the Israelis pick up guns, or the Poles or the Irish or any white man in the world says give me liberty or give me death, the entire white world applauds but when a black man says exactly the same thing, word for word, he is judged a criminal and treated like one and everything possible is done to make an example of [him] so there won't be any more like him."

During this period, the FBI had intensified their pursuit of Baldwin. On February 12, 1968, having searched the records of the Bureau of Vital Statistics (Marriage Records), they corrected a previous memo that claimed that Baldwin was married to Paula Baldwin, who was, in fact, his sister. Soon afterwards, they noted Baldwin's contract to write a film script about Malcolm X. In a memo on June 19, 1968, an FBI informant let them know that James Baldwin is "a Negro," as though this was news.

In August 1968, Baldwin spoke at a meeting of the Student National Coordinating Committee, previously the Student Nonviolent Coordinating Committee, whose tactics were milder than those of the Panthers. According to the FBI files, he "said he would not encourage his black brothers to go out & commit violence in the streets. Neither would he encourage them to stand by and let one of the brothers be hurt or killed. He warned his brothers not to be goaded into a fight on white man's soil and white man's terms. He said this could result in a whole generation of black activists being wiped out."

In April 1969, Baldwin was found by an agent returning from Mexico: "C said he was calling to advise BALDWIN had just arrived, at approximately 11–50am this date, at International Airport. He had been aboard Mexicana Airlines flight 906, from Mexico. He is presently checking his baggage through customs. C said he would call to advise any additional information, such as an address, if he got it later." In July, agents were authorized to purchase a book, *Black Anti-Semitism and Jewish Racism*, in which Baldwin had an essay.

Also in 1969, the FBI put together a typed summary of the information they had on Baldwin. This included an agent letting them know that in 1966 someone had "stated that the Northeast Louisiana State College at Monroe, Louisiana, made the book *Another World* by James Baldwin required reading. He advised the group that this book dealt with a Negro male making love to a White female. He suggested that Klansmen obtain copies of this book to determine whether it is suitable reading for college students."

In December 1969, the FBI translated an article about Baldwin in a Turkish newspaper in which he praised the country and its people and then, according to the FBI translation, went on to describe his own working habits: "There are times when he writes continuously for 24 hours without food and drink. Under such circumstances, he does not notice if you shout at him or hit him on the shoulder. Afterwards, he lies down and sleeps. Moreover, he is in a sound sleep for 48 hours. If you are able to awaken him, how fortunate you are."

In August 1972, when the FBI produced a summary of Baldwin's statements in an interview in the French magazine *L'Express*, he emerges as a radical Black thinker. When he mentioned how the Black population in America could, in the words of the translator, "destroy society," he was asked "In what way?" and replied—the FBI translation is fairly accurate here: "It is easy for us, for example, to make the cities uninhabitable. It is the Blacks who form the bulk of the urban services. In real estate, we are in the basement and the basement directs the life of the rest of the floors. It is very simple. In order to organize this type of resistance, it is not necessary to have a lot of people. And the war in Vietnam, in this regard, is very significant. That the most powerful country in the world, in twelve years, cannot manage to get the better of one of the poorest and most underdeveloped countries in the world, makes many Blacks wonder."

═══

Two weeks before he died, the poet W. B. Yeats wrote a poem called "Cuchulain Comforted," which began with a series of statements free of metaphor. The poem was written in *terza rima*, a form that was new for Yeats. Unusually, this poem did not need many drafts. It seems to have come to him easily, as if naturally. In earlier Yeats poems and plays, Cuchulain, a figure from Irish mythology, had appeared as the implacable, solitary, and violent hero, prepared for solo combat, free of fear. Now he has "six mortal wounds" and is attended by figures, Shrouds, who encourage him to join them in the act of sewing rather than fighting. They let him know that they themselves are not among the heroic dead but are "Convicted cowards all by kindred slain / Or driven from home and left to die in fear."

Thus, at the very end of his life, Yeats created an image which seemed the very opposite of what had often given vigor to his own imagination. His heroic figure has now been gentled; his fierce and solitary warrior has joined others in the act of sewing; instead of the company of brave men, Cuchulain seems content to rest finally among cowards.

This poem is not a culminating statement for Yeats, but a contradictory one; it is not a crowning version of a familiar poetic form, but an experiment in a form—*terza rima*—associated most with Dante. Instead of attempting to sum up, it is as though Yeats wished to release fresh energy by repudiating, by beginning again, by offering his hero a set of images alien to him, which served all the more to make the hero more unsettled, more ambiguous.

How fascinating to see a writer abandon bold self-assertion and, however briefly, find a tone that is compassionate and genial and tender.

Similarly, in much of V. S. Naipaul's writing there is a hauteur, a sense of personal grandeur. It does not trouble the great novelist to make judgments. But in a volume of letters between himself and his father when he, the son, was first living in England and his father was working as a journalist in Trinidad, and when both harbored literary ambitions, we see a rare vulnerability and a sympathy. These early letters allow us to see Naipaul as more entangled and haunted and complicated.

So, too, with Norman Mailer's depiction of Nicole, Gary Gilmore's girlfriend, in *The Executioner's Song*. It is not as though Nicole is portrayed merely as Mailer's opposite: thoughtful, modest, and often very quiet. Rather, she is imagined in full, given a complete life. None of her reactions or impulses can be easily predicted. Her desires change as do her responses to her circumstances. Her character is sometimes wayward and then loyal and steadfast. She takes some things lightly. She is one of the great literary creations. The fact that this must have involved an act of gargantuan self-suppression on the part of the author is hardly relevant.

In Joan Didion's two late, autobiographical works of memoir, *The Year of Magical Thinking* and *Blue Nights*, a more wounded version of the author's voice is evident. In her earlier collections of essays, and even in the novels, Didion's own style and the voices of her narrators used sharp, sudden insights and a strictly controlling intelligence to make sense of the world and the self. Even when she wrote about her own powerlessness, Didion sought a chiseled diction, and a staccato, first-person delivery, that suggested how carefully words and phrases had been chosen, how deliberately commas and full stops and paragraph breaks had been placed. All in the service of strength and judgment, offering a relentless insistence on Didion's own will, her own perspicacity.

In the books about the deaths of her husband and her daughter, on the other hand, Didion was like Naipaul with his father or Mailer with his strange, powerless heroine. She was alone, words failed her, words could not control anything— they must give way. What emerged was an anxious introspection. While once Didion had found patterns in reality and relished difficult truths, she was now at a loss. Nothing held. This late style of hers allowed us to read her earlier work in a different light.

There was, however, no such moment in Baldwin. From the beginning, he displayed his own vulnerability, his own softness, sometimes as a weapon but mostly as a way of transforming an argument so that it was not a contest to be won but rather a question to be reframed—to be moved from the narrow confines of the public realm back towards the self, the questing, uneasy spirit.

Baldwin did not need to move from bravery into a humbled self-realization, as in Yeats's poem, or to make peace with his father, as in Naipaul's letters, or to imagine and create a protagonist who did not share his privilege, as did Mailer, or to discover that his eloquence and sharp intelligence were, under pressure, no use at all, as did Didion.

Baldwin had lived with the knowledge of his own vulnerability from the beginning. It was the discovery of this that inspired him as a writer in the first place.

If there was one moment in Baldwin's work where we see him most clearly, it was in a piece he wrote about boxing. Baldwin, in general, had not much interest in violence. He didn't relish describing it. On the other hand, when he wrote about love, he tended to mean it.

How then could Baldwin write about two poor men fighting each other, to the delight of the crowd, in a boxing ring?

There is a myth that American writers have written with verve and originality about boxing. Boxing as elemental drama. Boxing as metaphor. Or boxing as the most important thing in the world. Or, as Joyce Carol Oates writes, "I can entertain the proposition that life is a metaphor for boxing . . . Life *is* like boxing in many unsettling respects. But boxing is only like boxing."

In 1938 Richard Wright wrote "High Tide in Harlem," an article about Joe Louis, for the left-wing magazine *New Masses*. When Louis won a fight against a German boxer, Wright reported from Harlem where "a hundred thousand black people surged out of taprooms, flats, restaurants, and filled the streets and sidewalks, like the Mississippi River overflowing in floodtime. With their faces to the night sky, they filled their lungs with air and let out a scream of joy that it seemed would never end, and a scream that seemed to come from untold reserves of strength."

The worst writer about boxing was Norman Mailer. His book *The Fight* contains many insanely bad phrases and sentences. "It was the time for each man to extort a measure of fear from the other. Liston had done it to all his opponents until he met Ali, who then Cassius Clay at the age of twenty-two, glared back at him with all the imperative of his high-destiny guts."

Would he not have glared with his eyes? In what way, were his guts "high-destiny"? And what does "all the imperative" mean? Would "some of the imperative" not be more accurate, if accuracy matters here?

Mailer moved from being a big boy relishing the violence ("Then he drove a lightning-strong right straight as a pole into the stunned center of Foreman's head") into pure banality ("Whatever else happened, Foreman had been hit").

Mailer resorted to animal imagery: horse, cat, bull, pumas, thoroughbred, tigers. He wrote about Muhammad Ali: "His eyes are as alive as a ghetto adolescent walking down a strange turf."

In 1962 when James Baldwin was commissioned by a magazine called *Nugget* to cover the boxing match in Chicago between Floyd Patterson and Sonny Liston, the press agent Harold Conrad remarked that Baldwin "doesn't know a left hook from a kick in the ass."

And this was true. That night, Baldwin was sitting near the ring beside Norman Mailer, who had recently reviewed Baldwin's novel *Another Country*. While he had managed to praise aspects of the novel, Mailer also wrote: "For the most part it is an abominably written book. It is sluggish in its prose, lifeless for its first hundred pages, stilted to despair in its dialogue." The two men had little to do with one another after that.

Baldwin saw Patterson and Liston less as marquee fighters or performers and more as two men engaged in the same survival struggle as so many others.

Before the match, in the company of the journalist Gay Talese, Baldwin visited Patterson in his private quarters. It is clear Baldwin was at a loss. He had no proper questions to ask the boxer. It would be easy to describe the way Baldwin observed Patterson as erotically charged—and it was—but more than that, Baldwin wondered about Patterson's inner life. This was, after all, what interested Baldwin most. He saw in Patterson "a terrible note of complexity" and "a style which strongly suggests that most un-American of attributes, privacy, the will to privacy." He imagined that Patterson "is still relentlessly, painfully shy . . . and while he has found a way to master this, he has found no way to hide it; as, for example, another miraculously tough and tender man, Miles Davis, has managed to do."

Patterson, Baldwin wrote, who is "tough and proud and beautiful, is also terribly vulnerable, and looks it."

This was tentative writing, untough, humble; the prose had none of the puffed-up vigor of other writers about boxing and boxers. Baldwin's interest in power and will and physical prowess was nothing compared to his concern about vulnerability which, in turn, became a way of seeing into the spirit of the man about whom he is writing. But he knew the limits of this. He really was not sure, and this was a useful stance in an arena where other writers were filled with certainty.

In the end, Baldwin wondered if it might be better if everyone left Patterson alone. "How would *I* like it if I were forced to answer inane questions every day concerning the progress of my work?"

What Baldwin mainly remembered was Patterson's voice and also "the glimpse I got of him then, a man more complex than he was yet equipped to know."

And then Baldwin was offered the chance of spending a small amount of time with Sonny Liston before the match. What he found in Liston was the same kind of softness he himself displayed as he wandered among these two fighters. "He reminded me of big, black men I have known who acquired the reputation of being tough in order to conceal the fact that they weren't hard."

This was not Baldwin offering a side of himself that is

scarcely apparent in his other essays or in his fiction. He had not suddenly become gentle. Instead, he was in a place where there was much temptation to write sharp, violent sentences and mimic action in his diction. It is lovely to watch Baldwin remaining himself.

And then he wrote a sentence about Liston that might have seemed ordinary, almost an afterthought. "Anyway, I liked him, liked him very much." This was not an encounter with journalist and boxer, but Baldwin exerting his humanity in a place where such exertions were scarce. He looked at Liston and tried to say something true.

He described Liston's face: "the curiously distant light in the eyes." He attempted to analyze Liston's silence. He saw him as inarticulate "in a particularly Negro way—he has a long tale to tell which no one wants to hear."

And then Baldwin himself, the most articulate of men, put aside his own rhetorical skills, and spoke to Liston: "I can't ask you any questions because everything's been asked. Perhaps I'm only here, really, to say that I wish you well."

Liston, he reported, "looked at me then, really for the first time, and he talked to me for a little while."

The Terror and
the Surrender

I am writing this in a second-floor apartment whose windows overlook Riverside Drive on the Upper West Side of New York City. Through the bare trees—it is winter—I can see the Hudson River. Later, at dusk, on good days, the color of the sky to the west turns into dramatic and elaborate pinks and reds.

Riverside Drive appears in James Baldwin's work. In *Another Country,* Rufus, his protagonist from Harlem, having played in a fashionable Harlem nightclub, goes to a party with a White woman whom he has met in the club. Baldwin has them in a taxi: "They were on Riverside Drive and nearing their destination. To the left of them, pale unlovely lights emphasized the blackness of the Jersey shore . . . Then the cab turned; he glimpsed, briefly, the distant bridge which glowed like something written in the sky."

The bridge is the George Washington.

In Baldwin's novel, it looms as large as it does in the actual landscape.

There is often an icy wind coming up from the river as you

turn from Broadway down 116th Street. It helps to know how much struggle is going on down there. As the Hudson attempts to make its way to the ocean, the tidal waters come up and hit against it. The water is moving in two directions.

I tried to write about this in a poem:

> The light's cut into pieces by bare trees
> And, below the lanes for traffic, the tide
> Flowing inland from the sea
> Hits the heavy currents of fresh water,
> Struggles, ducks under, loses its grip,
> Drowns in the Hudson, is drowning now.

A few years ago, I lived close by here in a top-floor apartment whose kitchen had a side window with a view of the George Washington Bridge. The bridge was lit up at night.

Sometimes, in these years away from home, random lines of poetry come into my head, including lines that my mother had learned and would say to herself; one or two lines, often the same ones.

A while ago, I was on a train leaving Paddington Station in London, going to Cheltenham. I was with a friend whose laptop, I noticed, was connected to the internet. Once the train was moving, two lines of poetry came into mind as though from nowhere, lines I must not have heard for maybe fifty years, lines recited by that voice, my mother's, in that kitchen in that house in Enniscorthy.

I asked my friend if he could possibly search to see what they were. I tried to recall the exact words:

That must be why the big things pass and the little
   things remain
Like the smell of the wattle at Lichtenberg
   [something] in the rain.

My mother said the words with a sort of sigh, like she said
lines from Yeats or lines from *Othello* and maybe other lines
that I have forgotten. She herself and her friends and her
sisters could talk naturally about what they thought *life* was,
and what it wasn't. My mother would often begin: "When you
have gone through *life* like I have . . ." Or say about a priest or
a Christian Brother: "They have no experience of *life*."

These poems that she remembered said something maybe
about *life*, something true, but also something unfathomable,
or she recited them because the words were beautiful and
mysterious, or created a feeling when you said them, a strange
emotion.

The lines I'd asked about on the train were, it turned out,
from a poem by Rudyard Kipling. They were a refrain in his
poem "Lichtenberg," from a set of poems published in 1903
in a volume called *Five Nations*, about the lives of soldiers on
duty. Lichtenberg is a town in South Africa. The narrator of
the poem is an Australian soldier. The poems opens: "Smells
are surer than sounds or sights / To make your heartstrings
crack," and its first stanza ends:

That must be why the big things pass
And the little things remain,
Like the smell of the wattle by Lichtenberg,
Riding in, in the rain.

I was going to Cheltenham. It was a Saturday morning. I had the newspapers on my lap. And this had come back out of the blue, or out of the maze of unforgotten things that carry strange emotion with them.

And it comes back again now as I work on the last chapter of this book.

One of the other set of lines my mother would say out loud comes from the South African poet Roy Campbell:

This mast, new-shaved, through whom I rive the ropes,
Says she was once an oread of the slopes

This makes me think of a day, a few weeks before the pandemic began, when I found a poem by Roy Campbell that was new to me. It was called "The Zulu Girl," about a mother breastfeeding a child. Its fourth stanza read thus:

Yet in that drowsy stream his flesh imbibes
An old unquenched, unsmotherable heat—
The curbed ferocity of beaten tribes,
The sullen dignity of their defeat.

For a moment, I felt almost indignant that a poem had been used to air these prejudices. Did Campbell really mean to suggest that she, as a Zulu, had been defeated, was a member of a "beaten tribe"? Beaten by whom? The White South Africans? No one, I thought, would write that now. Instead, I suppose, they would think it, bottle it up, air it in other ways. It is probably foolish to think that poetry should be free of such bigotry.

Letting my mind wander, I thought of other lines by other

poets that made me uneasy. What about the second stanza of
A. D. Hope's "Australia"?

They call her a young country, but they lie:
She is the last of lands, the emptiest,
A woman beyond her change of life, a breast
Still tender but within the womb is dry.

Or the four final lines of Louis Simpson's "To the Western
World":

In this America, this wilderness
Where the axe echoes with a lonely sound,
The generations labor to possess
And grave by grave we civilize the ground.

Grave by grave, *we do what?* Maybe Louis Simpson was joking.

In 1962, Simpson, who was born in Jamaica in 1923, published a novel called *Riverside Drive*, which used elements of
his own life. He had studied at Columbia University so he must
have known these streets. His protagonist Duncan Bell must
have walked below my window at a time when, as Simpson
wrote in the novel, "the trees had put on all their leaves; a
summer wind blew from the Jersey side, where docks and fac-
tories huddled along the water. On the edge of the Palisades
an enlarged crimson sun was going down."

And there is another old ghost whom I must have passed
several times. In that funny hour on winter afternoons when
the sky is blue and the light is clear and "the world, Riverside
Drive, was wickedly lighted up," as Saul Bellow writes in his

novel *Mr. Sammler's Planet*, I pass the vivid spirit of Bellow's eponymous hero Mr. Minutely-Observant Artur Sammler, as Bellow calls him. He is unstately, tall, aging, as he makes his way home to his apartment, a block away from here.

Sammler is so observant in the first chapter of Bellow's novel that he notices a man, a Black man, who, at Columbus Circle, gets on the bus that goes to Riverside Drive. The man is a pickpocket. His face "showed the effrontery of a big animal," the novel tells us. Sometime later, the same man follows Mr. Sammler and confronts him in the lobby of his building on Riverside Drive. But not to assault him, rather to show Mr. Sammler his erect penis, "a large tan-and-purple uncircumcised thing—a tube, a snake."

The man does not speak. "He was never to hear the black man's voice."

I have been for a walk and watched the surface ice on the road and the park walkway brightened by the last rays of sunlight and then by the unlovely street lights. In a few minutes the sun will be gone altogether.

I am glad I went for a walk because, when I returned and read over what I had written above, I realized how ungenerous some of it is. The short quotes chosen from poems by Roy Campbell, A. D. Hope, and Louis Simpson, and from Saul Bellow's novel, serve to demonstrate how prejudiced these men, or the personae they created, could be, how strange some of their thoughts and images were.

What are we meant to do with such infringements of what we might call decency? Why did I select these quotes and put them so self-righteously on display?

I came across the work of Roy Campbell first when I read his haunting and beautiful translations of St. John of the Cross. When I was in my late teens, I went to a lecture about Australian literature and heard a poem by A. D. Hope recited. I searched for his work and admired its elegance, its formal perfections, and I still do. I know Louis Simpson for his poems about his own experience as an American soldier in the Second World War.

And, even still, after half a century reading him, I still get immense pleasure and satisfaction from the work of Saul Bellow—his comic dissatisfaction at how the world is ordered and disordered.

How shameful then to find myself policing the work of these four men.

In 1954, Saul Bellow wrote a subtle and thoughtful report on James Baldwin's application, which was successful, for a Guggenheim award. He referred to Baldwin's "wisdom and talent." He went on: "For the most part, the Whites have hitherto dealt with individual Negroes as representative of their race—as social types. Mr. Baldwin makes a special bid to be considered as an individual—to have all men considered so. He approaches the matter as an artist and social historian: first as an artist."

Baldwin was also, of course, a teacher. He read the world and the text with care. In his writing, he showed us how to notice and taught us to interpret as though from an angle. I take from his writing a cast of mind. He believed that the argument begins and ends with love, and the large and unwieldy part in-between requires rage, ironic treatment, and an ethical framework. Life amused him as much as it appalled him. Baldwin saw no reason to take himself entirely seriously. He had an eye for what was ridiculous. But then, at certain moments, he soared into a pure seriousness.

I can't imagine the scorn he would pour on some Irishman sitting helplessly in some apartment on Riverside Drive policing some poems as well as a passage from Saul Bellow and then thinking better of it. He would shake his head in puzzlement. He himself had more interesting things to consider, such as the ways in which masculinity and race can be presented in a novel, and how much work he put into the idea of the private life in his novel *Another Country*.

In the short fiction he wrote after *Go Tell It on the Mountain*, Baldwin sought to dramatize ideas of male strength and weakness in both the North and the South, in the lives of both African American and White people.

In the collection of stories *Going to Meet the Man*, there are two stories about men. One man is White and from the South; the other is African American and from Harlem. One story is called "Going to Meet the Man," and the other is "Sonny's Blues." Together, they show Baldwin's imagination as polarized, more capable of making images of opposites than making connections. In both stories, he is interested once more in the concept of the private life.

Baldwin saw how racism in America had maimed private life, had entered into the spirit of people—White as much as Black—and defaced their dreams. He sought a reimagining of the private realm, and one way of pursuing this was in fiction, a place that gives sanctuary to nuance, the half-said, the unsayable, the unimaginable, the shameful, the image bathed in glory or pathos or in some ambiguous state in-between the two.

The American South was not Baldwin's territory as Harlem was. Even though he had an acute sense of Southern racism not merely as an injustice but as evil, this lived with him as an idea, one that he could discuss in his essays, but he did not have enough personal knowledge of the South to set his novels there. He could easily and powerfully imagine the Southern past, as experienced by his parents, but not the present moment. Sometimes, in his dreams, he was an insider there; in reality, he was an outsider.

The story "Going to Meet the Man" is set in the South during the civil rights era. It is written from the point of view of a White sheriff who in the first lines of the story makes his sexual interest in Black women clear, and then goes on to muse on the Black boy he has arrested and brutally assaulted, and the lynching, described in lengthy and unbearable detail, which his father took him to when he was a child. Thinking of the lynching excites him sexually. Since the story opens with him not being able to perform sexually, this is rectified by the end as he contemplates racial violence of the most horrific sort.

The story belongs to the rage of its moment. Its tone is inflammatory, as the story seeks to connect racist violence with sexual excitement—as it tries to connect the most vile public images and the most private urges. The story offers us the sheriff's lack of humanity as a demonstration of Baldwin's views on race and sex and violence and the South. Clearly, this was not a time for distance from the burning world.

Writing about the North, on the other hand, allowed Baldwin to describe the private life with tenderness and suggestiveness. In *Go Tell It on the Mountain*, there is a great difference between John and his half-brother Roy, who "had often disappeared between Sunday school and morning service and had not come back all day." Later, in the story "Sonny's Blues," the tension is between the narrator, who is a teacher and a solid man, and his brother Sonny, who is wayward and a jazz pianist. The narrator remembers his brother's "great gentleness and privacy." When he is older, Sonny "looked out from the depths of his private life, like an animal waiting to be coaxed into the light." Although Sonny and his father had many differences, "they both had—that same privacy."

It is clear that Sonny is doomed, but Baldwin dramatizes the fact that this is not his only story. Like "Going to Meet the Man," at its core "Sonny's Blues" has images of racist brutality, less graphic but all the more haunting for that. What is most haunting in "Sonny's Blues," however, is what most redeems Sonny. He is presented as a complex man with a complex life, a life that emerges fiercely and plaintively in the last pages as the narrator describes his brother playing piano, music being for him "personal, private, vanishing evocations," in a band led by a bass player called Creole.

In the last pages of the story, Baldwin let the description of the music soar:

> And Sonny went all the way back, he really began with the spare, flat statement of the opening phrase of the song. Then he began to make it his. It was very beautiful because it wasn't hurried and it was no longer a lament. I seemed to hear with what burning he had made it his, with what burning he had yet to make it ours, how we could cease lamenting. Freedom lurked around us and I understood, at last, that he could help us to be free if we would listen, that we would never be free until we did.

The sound here is as restrained and cool as the notes being described. The pacing is sure because it has paid attention to the actual music and has taken a lesson from this that is anything but simple. The player could only "help" us to be free, that was all, but the main image here is mysterious, suggesting a sound that was "no longer a lament" in a time when there was so much to be sorrowful about and so much to put anyone into a rage. The music did not heal, nor did the prose, but indicated a way.

It is unlikely that Baldwin could have managed such sentences in the South where he was, before anything else, an appalled witness. "Sonny's Blues" is set in Harlem and Harlem was home. Harlem was not only North to the American South, but it was North to Greenwich Village. And it was that axis, connected by the A train, that now began to interest Baldwin.

In 1985 in an essay called "Here Be Dragons," Baldwin remembered his time in the Village after the death of his father:

> There were very few black people in the Village in those years, and of that handful, I was decidedly the most improbable . . . I was eager, vulnerable and lonely . . . I am sure that I was afraid that I already seemed and sounded too much like a woman. In my childhood, at least until my adolescence, my playmates had called me a sissy . . . On every street corner, I was called a faggot.

Baldwin lived on the Lower East Side when he came back from his first extended trip to the South. "While in the South I had suppressed my terror well enough, in any case, to function; but when the pressure came off, a kind of wonder of terror overcame me, making me as useless as a snapped rubber band."

Baldwin had made the journey back north, only to find himself lost. It is this sense of displacement that created the figure of Rufus in the opening chapter, almost ninety pages in length, of *Another Country*, his third novel, published in 1962.

The gap between North and South in *Another Country*, between Harlem and the Village, is even more tense and fraught and dangerous than the gap between North and South in Baldwin's essays. For Rufus, Harlem is home and he does not want to go back there. Not now; not yet. He has imagined his way into a new place, what Baldwin might call a private place, where he will seek to have a private life. The demons who haunt him will be private ones, emerging as disturbed inner energy. Rufus is not a victim. But his autonomy that seems large in the novel is in fact restricted.

Another Country deals with masculinity and race and rage and the fate of Rufus, the young musician from Harlem who had dared to live in Greenwich Village. Rufus has felt hatred and been brushed by its wings, but Baldwin is too subtle and alert to the danger of making him merely angry. Rufus's new friends in the Village are White. In an essay written in 1960 called "Notes for a Hypothetical Novel," Baldwin mused on the White people he met in downtown New York in his early twenties:

> In the beginning, I thought that the white world was very different from the world I was moving out of and I turned out to be entirely wrong . . . But I didn't meet anyone in that world who didn't suffer from the same affliction that all the people I had fled from suffered from and that was that they didn't know who they were. They wanted to be someone that they were not.

Baldwin made Rufus bad as well as brilliant; he placed a violent and self-destructive charm at the core of him. And he made Rufus's White friends uneasy figures, unable to protect themselves from their own longings and insecurities. But Rufus stands apart from them, not trusting of their motives for wanting him and liking him.

In 1960 in his essay "Alas, Poor Richard," Baldwin alluded to the "body of sexual myths . . . around the figure of the American Negro," who "is penalized for the guilty imagination of the white people who invest him with their hates and longings, and is the principal target of their sexual longings." Rufus is aware of this and suspicious of his own attractions. He will grow to hate the White woman who wants him. He will grow to despise and distrust his White friends. He will eventually walk the city, destitute and forlorn. He will do what Baldwin's friend Eugene Worth did in 1946: he will finally jump to his death off the George Washington Bridge.

———

Rufus "was in the novel," Baldwin said, "because I don't think anyone had ever watched the disintegration of a black boy from that particular point of view. Rufus was partly responsible for his doom."

In creating Rufus, Baldwin was seeking to "break out of the whole sentimental image" of the hero from Harlem driven to suicide by White people.

Rufus is a tragic hero caught between the time when men such as him had no freedom and a possible time to come. The city has opened its doors to him, but not enough for him to feel free, just enough for him to feel danger and threat. He is like someone who has been released from solitary confinement into the wider prison. He is the figure whom Baldwin saw that he himself might have become.

Two years after the suicide of his friend Eugene Worth, Baldwin left New York and moved to Paris. "I didn't know what was going to happen to me in Paris," he told the *Paris Review*, "but I knew what was going to happen to me in New York. If I had stayed there, I would have gone under, like my friend on the George Washington Bridge."

He wrote Rufus, then, as a shadow version of himself, with some of his own soulful charm. He made him a drummer and he gave him not only a complicated inner life and an intricate and nuanced way of noticing and remembering, but also, like Sonny in "Sonny's Blues," a way of creating beauty once night fell and there were other musicians around. This is, for Baldwin, private life at its most intense.

Rufus remembers being onstage with a saxophone player who

> took off on a terrific solo . . . The silence of the listeners became strict with abruptly focused attention, cigarettes were unlit, and drinks stayed on the tables; and in all of the faces, even the most ruined and most dull, a curious wary light appeared. They were being assaulted by the saxophonist who perhaps no longer wanted their love and merely hurled his outrage at them with the same contemptuous, pagan pride with which he humped the air. And yet the question was terrible and real; the boy was blowing with his lungs and guts out of his own short past.

Baldwin can infuse the most simple phrase here, such as "and drinks stayed on the tables," with a suggestive meaning. He can use words like "light" and "love" and "outrage" and "contemptuous" and "pagan" and "pride" with the confidence of someone who has been schooled in the language of sermons.

Compare this passage with a description of a bar downtown where Rufus goes in the company of his White friends:

> The bar was terribly crowded. Advertising men were there drinking double shots of bourbon or vodka, on the rocks; college boys were there, their wet fingers slippery on the beer bottles; lone men stood near the doors or in corners, watching the drifting women. The college boys, gleaming with ignorance and mad with chastity, made terrified efforts to attract the feminine attention, but succeeded only in attracting each other. Some of the men were buying drinks for some of the women—who wandered incessantly from the jukebox to the bar—and they faced each other over smiles which were pitched, with an eerie precision, between longing and contempt. Black-and-white couples were together here—closer together now than they would be later, when they got home. These several histories were camouflaged in the jargon which, wave upon wave, rolled through the bar; were locked in a silence like the silence of glaciers. Only the juke box spoke, grinding out each evening, all evening long, syncopated, synthetic laments for love.

Here, too, there is music, but it is "synthetic." Here, too, there are drinks, but they make no one happy. Here, too, there is contempt, but it is not the "contemptuous, pagan pride," the phrase used to describe the virtuosity of a musician playing.

The first passage shows Baldwin building an inner life for Rufus, a sanctuary in which there is mystery and passion and a fiercely guarded privacy. The second describes what is garish and sad, utterly lonely. The first passage is all redemption; the second is one in which redemption is neither sought nor offered. It is from the second that Rufus will flee. He will move north where home once was, but now he will move towards death and self-destruction.

Soon, in the second chapter of the book, Rufus's sister Ida will make the journey south, from Harlem to the Village. Ida will come with the fervor of Antigone to ask the question: "Where is my brother?" She will come south with a tone that is unforgiving, relentless. Part of the power she has is that she comes from a place no one in the Village knows. It may be on the same small island, but it could not be further away.

These are the distances that interest Baldwin, the ones that cannot be easily measured nor bridged. He journeyed to the South in his fiction so that he could see the North more clearly, but, by the time he made it back to the North, it was the journey itself that mattered more. And that journey stood mostly as a metaphor for a journey Baldwin cared about, which was the spiritual journey, the journey inwards that he allowed the characters in his fiction to make as they themselves moved from simple optimism or predetermined doom into a state of complexity that could only be reconciled in moments, moments when all seemed ready to heal. And yet these moments are often in the past and they haunt a present that Baldwin was ready to face with as much clarity as he could summon up, and with some foreboding.

In the early pages of *Another Country*, as we watch Rufus and Leona seducing each other, Baldwin's ear for speech offers him great possibilities for expression and drama. Rufus is cool and sexy and understated; his speech carries sharp and streetwise self-confidence. But in the background all the time there is an ominous undersound. The opening pages let us know how close to the end Rufus is, and even in the passages where Rufus is high on life, there are always snatches of doom-laden memory or images of darkness. Rufus's self-invention, and his joy at the night and the party and the company and the sex, are all thin and will not last.

Baldwin had thought carefully about what to do in fiction with a figure like Rufus. He resisted the temptation to have Rufus, who is so lovable, so innocent, and so full of rage, made into a public martyr. Baldwin wanted the danger to come from within. He knew that for Rufus this was where the danger lay.

Baldwin began with the characters of Ida and Vivaldo (Vivaldo in earlier drafts had been Black), "but I couldn't find a way to make you understand Ida," he told the *Paris Review*. "Then Rufus came along and the entire action made sense."

Baldwin used the city he knew, especially in his late teens, the years after his father's death, when at the edge of poverty and despair he moved from job to job. He used small events such as his brother's teeth being knocked out by a White officer in the Navy, and himself and some friends being beaten up in a bar. He also used details which had nothing to do with his own background or his own experiences but had to do with certain situations and atmospheres he was soaking up: *Another Country* has some of the darkness and sense of gloom you get in French fiction and philosophy of that period, and it is also full of the pessimism and claustrophobia of Ingmar Bergman's films. Baldwin admired Bergman; he went to Stockholm to interview him and they became friends.

Another Country is the book where Baldwin's two most notable selves meet each other. There seems to be a large gap between the world of *Go Tell It on the Mountain*, which is, on the surface, settled and conservative and religious, and the world of *Giovanni's Room*, which is wandering and venal. Just as there seemed to be light-years between Baldwin's Harlem childhood and Baldwin's life in Paris. But his first two novels share a concern with the flesh, with moral questions and dramatic possibilities around carnality and sensuality. In his third novel, Baldwin introduces the two worlds to each other, bringing Rufus and Ida down from Harlem to a world of bohemians and writers; he mixes and matches the two worlds he himself lived in and understood.

All of his characters suffer from a longing for a purer love, or even the beginning of one; all of them, too, are desperately weak and capable of destruction.

———

In all three of these novels, Baldwin lets two very powerful ideas play against each other. One can be traced in his essays, which suggest that America is seriously deformed as a society because it cannot accept a large minority of its population and therefore cannot accept itself. By its treatment of the Black population, it has managed to disable itself. Thus, any group of people in any American novel must reflect this. Baldwin's other idea redeems him from being merely a critic of America in his novels; this idea proposes that life itself is dark, that relationships are fraught and broken, and personalities are destructive because of the way we are made.

Baldwin's novels combine a criticism of life that is essentially political with one which is philosophical. And because he is interested in his characters who are trapped in life, rather than life in the abstract or as a mere concept, the novels take on a menacing, dramatic, and engrossing power.

None of this explains the structure of *Another Country*. Rufus is Baldwin's Hamlet, and the novel allows Rufus to disappear early in the book. He is replaced by Ida, his sister. "The principal action in the book, for me," Baldwin told the *Paris Review*, "is the journey of Ida and Vivaldo toward some kind of coherence . . . You never go into her mind, but I had to make you see what is happening to this girl by making you feel the blow of her brother's death—the key to her relationship with everybody. She tries to make everybody pay for it. You cannot do that, life is not like that, you only destroy yourself."

The scene where Ida first appears in the novel, filtered through Cass's inquiring and sympathetic eye, is Baldwin at his most Jamesian, every moment offering a new angle and a new clue to nuance of character. Baldwin can also replace Rufus with another version of himself, his Laertes back from abroad, in the guise of Eric. And he can dramatize moments from his own life with his Swiss lover Lucien Happersberger, whom he had met in Paris and who later came to New York, as well as describe the lives of writers and would-be writers in Greenwich Village.

Baldwin had grown fascinated not only by the drama of

Black versus White, but by the drama of masculinity. Thus, while the first part of *Another Country* deals with the erotics of race and its discontents, after the death of Rufus the novel allows Baldwin to deal with the confines and conflicts of gender by which all his characters are so disturbed.

In 1985, two years before his death, Baldwin published his essay "Freaks and the American Idea of Manhood," in which he wrote: "The American *ideal*, then, of sexuality appears to be rooted in the American ideal of masculinity. This appeal has created cowboys and Indians, good guys and bad guys, punks and studs, tough guys and softies, butch and faggot, black and white. It is an ideal so paralytically infantile that it is virtually forbidden—as an unpatriotic act—that the American boy evolve into the complexity of manhood."

Baldwin's version of the American dream hangs just as grimly over his other characters as over Rufus and Leona. Masculinity is a nightmare from which his characters cannot awake. The city is a prison-house of desires that cannot be fulfilled.

"Richard and Cass," Baldwin told the *Paris Review*, "were part of the décor. From my point of view there was nothing in the least idealistic about Richard. He was modelled on several liberal American careerists from then and now." Vivaldo, more than any of the other characters, is locked in the world of Benno's bar, pitched between longing and contempt, stuck inside an icy masculinity.

The second part of the novel dramatizes Vivaldo's efforts to escape from this. The key moment in his slow and uneasy redemption occurs in the scene where he has been watching a blonde woman at the bar and he moves into a sort of rev-erie—a way of seeing a hard freedom won, in a place where distinctions fade—that animated Baldwin's imagination all his life, and became his credo:

> And something in him was breaking: he was briefly and horribly, in a region where there were no definitions of any kind, neither of color nor of male or female. There was only the leap and the rending and the terror and the surrender.

Acknowledgments

I am grateful to Brandeis University, and especially to Professor Ramie Targoff, for the invitation to deliver the Mandel Lectures in 2022. Thanks also to Professor Ulka Anjaria at Brandeis for her kindness and hospitality, as well as Diana Filar and Bailey Ludwig.

At Brandeis University Press, I wish to thank Sue Berger Ramin, the director, and also Jim Schley for his painstaking work on the manuscript, and for his many inspired and helpful suggestions and comments.

I want also to acknowledge editors who have published some of my writing about James Baldwin over the past twenty-five years, most notably Mary Kay Wilmers at the *London Review of Books*, Brendan Barrington at the *Dublin Review*, and the late Robert Silvers at the *New York Review of Books*.

Over these years, I had many conversations about Baldwin with my friend Eileen Ahearn, who died in January 2023. I will be forever grateful for her insights and her encouragement.

Thanks to Robinson Murphy for his suggestions and comments on the manuscript.

Also, thanks to Catriona Crowe, Hedi El Kholti, Ed Mulhall, Fintan O'Toole, and James Shapiro. And to Julia Bannon and Amin Stambuli. And to my agent Peter Straus for his careful reading of the book.

Selected
Bibliography

Works by James Baldwin

BOOKS

Another Country. New York: Dial Press, 1962.

Evidence of Things Not Seen. New York: Holt, 1985.

The Fire Next Time. New York: Dial Press, 1963.

Giovanni's Room. New York: Dial Press, 1956.

Going to Meet the Man. New York: Dial Press, 1965.

Go Tell It on the Mountain. New York: Alfred A. Knopf, 1953.

Nobody Knows My Name. New York: Dial Press, 1961.

No Name in the Street. New York: Dial Press, 1972.

Notes of a Native Son. Boston: Beacon Press, 1955.

The Price of the Ticket: Collected Nonfiction 1948–1985. New York: St. Martin's Press, 1985.

ESSAYS

"Alas, Poor Richard." *Le Preuve,* 1961.

"A Question of Identity." *Partisan Review,* July/August 1954.

"As Much Truth as One Can Bear." *New York Times Book Review,*
    January 14, 1962.

"The Discovery of What It Means to Be an American." *New York*
    Times Book Review, January 25, 1959.

"Down at the Cross." *New Yorker,* November 9, 1962.

"Everybody's Protest Novel." In *Notes of a Native Son.* Boston: Bea-
    con Press, 1955.

"Freaks and the American Ideal of Manhood." *Playboy,* January 1985.

"Here Be Dragons." In *The Price of the Ticket: Collected Nonfiction*
    1948–1985. New York: St. Martin's Press, 1985.

"Nobody Knows My Name: A Letter from the South." In *Nobody*
    Knows My Name. New York: Dial Press, 1961.

"Notes for a Hypothetical Novel." In *Nobody Knows My Name.* New
    York: Dial Press, 1961.

"Notes of a Native Son." *Harper's Magazine,* November 1955.

"Sonny's Blues." *Partisan Review,* Summer 1957.

"The Fight: Patterson vs. Liston." *Nugget,* February 1963.

"The Harlem Ghetto." In *Notes of a Native Son.* Boston: Beacon
    Press, 1955.

"The Outing." *New Story,* April 1951.

"The Rockpile." In *Going to Meet the Man.* New York: Dial Press, 1965.

"The White Problem." In *100 Years of Emancipation.* Edited by Rob-
    ert A. Goldwin. Chicago: Rand McNally, 1964.

"This Morning, This Evening, So Soon." *Atlantic Monthly,* Septem-
    ber 1960.

Secondary Sources

Banim, John, and Michael Banim. *The Croppy: A Tale of 1798*. London: H. Colburn, 1828.

Bellow, Saul. *Mister Sammler's Planet*. New York: Viking, 1964.

———. *Saul Bellow: Letters*. Edited by Benjamin Taylor. New York: Viking, 2020.

Boland, Eavan. "The Lost Art of Letter Writing." *New Yorker*, August 25, 2014.

Boyd, Herb. *Baldwin's Harlem: A Biography of James Baldwin*. New York: Atria, 2008.

Campbell, James. *Talking at the Gates: A Life of James Baldwin*. Berkeley: University of California Press, 2002.

Campbell, Roy. "Choosing a Mast" and "The Zulu Girl." In *Selected Poems*. London: Bodley Head, 1968.

Clarke, John Henrik, editor and introduction. *Harlem U.S.A.: The Story of a City within a City*. Brooklyn: A & B Books, 1971.

Cleaver, Eldridge. *Soul on Ice*. New York: McGraw-Hill, 1967.

Cullen, Countee. "To France." In *Collected Poems*. Edited by Major Jackson. New York, Library of America, 2013.

Didion, Joan. *Blue Nights*. New York: Knopf, 2011.

———. *The Year of Magical Thinking*. New York: Knopf, 2005.

Eliot, T. S. "Tradition and the Individual Talent." In *Selected Prose*. Edited by Frank Kermode. New York: Ecco, 2023.

Forster, E. M. *Maurice*. London: Edward Arnold, 1971.

Greenberg, Cheryl. *"Or Does It Explode?": Black Harlem in the Great Depression*. Oxford: Oxford University Press, 1997.

Griffin, Farah Jasmine. *"Who Set You Flowin'?": The African-American Migration Novel*. New York: Oxford University Press, 1995.

Griffin, John Howard. *Black Like Me.* New York: New American Library, 2010.

Hemingway, Ernest. *The Sun Also Rises.* In *Ernest Hemingway: Works.* Edited by Malcolm Cowley. New York: Viking, 1944.

Hope, A. D. "Australia." In *Collected Poems: 1930–1965.* New York: Viking, 1967.

James, Henry. *The Ambassadors* and *The Golden Bowl.* In *Henry James: Novels 1903–1911.* New York: Library of America, 2011.

Johnson, James Weldon. *Black Manhattan.* In *Writings.* New York: Library of America, 2004.

Kipling, Rudyard. *A Choice of Kipling's Verse Made by T. S. Eliot.* Edited and introduced by T. S. Eliot. Garden City, NY: Anchor, 1962.

Leeming, David. *James Baldwin: A Biography.* New York: Arcade, 2015.

Lester, Julius. "James Baldwin: Reflections of a Maverick." *New York Times Book Review,* May 27, 1984.

Mailer, Norman. *The Executioner's Song.* New York: Vintage, 1979.

———. *The Fight.* Boston: Little, Brown, 1975.

McKay, Claude. *A Long Way from Home.* New York: Harcourt, Brace and World, 1970.

Mead, Margaret, and James Baldwin. *A Rap on Race.* New York: Lippincott, 1971.

Naipaul, V. S. *Between Father and Son: Family Letters.* New York: Knopf, 2000.

Obama, Barack. *The Audacity of Hope: Thoughts on Reclaiming the American Dream.* New York: Crown, 2006.

———. *Dreams from My Father: A Story of Race and Inheritance.* New York: Random House, 1994.

Report of the National Advisory Commission on Civil Disorders. Introduction by Tom Wicker. New York: Dutton, 1968.

Simpson, Louis. *Riverside Drive.* New York: Atheneum, 1962.

———. "To the Western World." In *The Owner of the House: New Collected Poems 1940–2001.* Rochester, NY: BOA Editions, 2003.

Smith, William Gardner. *The Stone Face.* Introduction by Adam Shatz. New York: New York Review Books, 2021.

Trilling, Lionel. "On James Baldwin's *Another Country.*" *Mid-Century,* September 1962.

Walcott, Derek. "The Schooner Flight." In *The Star-Apple Kingdom.* New York: Farrar, Straus and Giroux, 1979.

Wilde, Oscar. *De Profundis.* London: Methuen, 1905.

Wilkerson, Isabel. *The Warmth of Other Suns: The Epic Story of America's Great Migration.* New York: Random House, 2010.

Wright, Richard. *Black Boy (American Hunger).* In *Richard Wright: Later Works.* New York: Library of America, 2011.

———. "High Tide in Harlem: Joe Louis as a Symbol of Freedom." *New Masses,* July 5, 1938.

Yeats, W. B. "Cuchulain Comforted." In *Collected Poems of W. B. Yeats.* New York: Macmillan, 1979.

The MANDEL LECTURES

in the HUMANITIES

at BRANDEIS UNIVERSITY

*Sponsored by the Jack, Joseph and
Morton Mandel Foundation*

DIRECTOR, PROFESSOR ULKA ANJARIA

The Mandel Lectures in the Humanities were launched in the fall of 2011 to promote humanistic inquiry at Brandeis University, following the 2010 opening of the new Mandel Center for the Humanities. The lectures bring to the Mandel Center each year an influential scholar or scholar-practitioner who gives a series of lectures on topics of broad interest for a range of campus audiences. The Mandel Lectures are unique in their celebration of cutting-edge topics, forms, and modes of inquiry in the arts, humanities, and humanistic social sciences: the speakers have ranged from historians and literary critics to performance artists, writers, and anthropologists. The published series of books reflects the interdisciplinary mission of the center and the wide range of extraordinary work being done in the humanities today.

*For a complete list of books that are available in the series,
visit https://brandeisuniversitypress.com/series/mandel-lectures.*

About the Author

———

Colm Tóibín is the author of eleven novels, including *Long Island* and *The Magician*, as well as two story collections and several books of criticism. He is the Irene and Sidney B. Silverman Professor of the Humanities at Columbia University and has been named the 2022–2024 Laureate for Irish Fiction by the Arts Council of Ireland.